Be Gentle,
Be Faithful

Daily Meditations
for Busy Christians

James Stephen Behrens, OCSO

ACTA
ASSISTING CHRISTIANS TO ACT
PUBLICATIONS

Dedicated to my twin brother
Gregory James

Be Gentle, Be Faithful
Daily Meditations for Busy Christians
by James Stephen Behrens, OCSO

Jeffrey Paul Behrens took the name James Stephen when he entered the Monastery of the Holy Spirit in Conyers, Georgia. Fr. Behrens was ordained in the Archdiocese of Newark, New Jersey, where he worked for over twenty years before joining the Trappists.

Edited by Patrice J. Tuohy and Gregory F. Augustine Pierce
Cover design by Tom A. Wright
Design and Typesetting by Garrison Publications

Published by: ACTA Publications
　　　　　　　 Assisting Christians To Act
　　　　　　　 4848 N. Clark Street
　　　　　　　 Chicago, IL 60640
　　　　　　　 773-271-1030

Library of Congress Catalog Number: 99-65633

ISBN: 0-87946-209-4

Printed in the United States of America

99 00 01 02 03 Year/Printing 8 7 6 5 4 3 2 1

Time to Embrace Time

New Year's Day is very low keyed at the monastery. No fireworks. No hangovers. No waving good-bye to the old and kissing the new. It is a day like any other day, a nice day to befriend time. So I sit in the woods here in Georgia and hope I take to heart the good things this year will bring.

Colossians 4:5

Conduct yourselves wisely toward outsiders, making the most of the time.

BE IT RESOLVED

If you goofed up on any New Year's resolutions, do not be hard on yourself. Make one more resolution: forgive yourself. From that forgiveness, forgive others their failed resolutions. Be at peace with yourself and everybody else.

ROMANS **14:13**

Let us therefore no longer pass judgment on one another, but resolve instead never to put a stumbling block or hindrance in the way of another.

THE HEART

Alberto Rios is a novelist and short story writer and teacher of creative writing. He is aware of how cowed young people can be when they try to write a story. Their heads are too filled with techniques, plot variations, fears of all sorts, inhibitions, and too many previous lessons.

In his first class he asks that they suspend all preconceived ideas and concentrate on one simple thing for the duration of the course: a tea cup and nothing else. He wants them to write about the tea cup. On first hearing this the students scoff. But he is insistent that they try to banish every other thought from their minds when it comes time to write. Let the cup teach you, he tells them. Most students oblige, and after a few weeks they get the point. Simplicity comes to the fore and the stories submitted show a remarkable diversity born from faithfulness to a simple cup.

Humans have only one heart, and how burdened that heart can become with fears and worries, regrets and sorrows. Yet it is with heart that we see, love, enjoy, remember, hope, and grow.

In taking all things to heart we are in turn given insight into them, as often and as deeply as we like.

PSALM **49:3**

My mouth shall speak wisdom;
the meditation of my heart
shall be understanding.

THE CLOSE OF DAY

The last pastor I worked under used to wait up for me if I was out late to a meeting or visiting friends. When I pulled into the rectory parking lot, I would sometimes see him standing at the door. He would wave as I passed and then go into the living room and wait. On especially late evenings, he would retire but would often leave a little something on my chair: a friendly note, a gift, some candies. Such kindness came naturally to him.

I miss this priest. His kindnesses made an enormous difference in how I remember him and the home we shared. Rarely do I see a lit window in the evening without his image, waiting for me at the close of a day, coming to mind.

When I pray, I speak to a God I have never met, a God who at times seems far away. But I like to think that God waits for us all with love, looking from every window or doorway that is made holy through human loving by those who, like my friend, wait.

MATTHEW 5:16

"In the same way, let your light shine before others, so that they may see your good works and give glory to your Father in heaven."

The Man by the Sea

He had lost ones he loved at sea. A jet had fallen into the ocean. There were no survivors. He parked his van and walked slowly toward the surf and stopped when he reached the water. He looked out over the ocean. Then he leaned down, cupped his hand and took some water from the sea, raised it to his lips, and kissed it. He poured the water back into the surf, turned, and walked away.

A reporter saw the man and later wrote about it. His grief and gesture were sacred and powerful. He kissed the water that buried part of his heart beneath its waves. He kissed the water that sustained so many living things, but not the ones he loved. The water would not or could not give them back. But his kiss was gentle, sad yet forgiving. The man returned to his van, his hands and lips moist with life, his heart sore to the point of breaking.

The man's grief was shared by millions who read that reporter's article. When life is lost, everyone loses.

Revelation 7:17

> "For the Lamb at the center of the
>   throne will be their shepherd,
> and he will guide them to springs of
>   the water of life,
> and God will wipe away every tear from
>   their eyes."

Epiphany

A star moves, wise men travel far, messages are given in dreams, a child is adored and offered precious gifts, and truth is revealed through a babe born in a manger—so the story goes. Some say it is all a myth, but history is best understood by following the hopes and dreams of the human heart.

Matthew 2:10-11

When they saw that the star had stopped, they were overwhelmed with joy. On entering the house, they saw the child with Mary his mother; and they knelt down and paid him homage. Then, opening their treasure chests, they offered him gifts of gold, frankincense, and myrrh.

Barn Cat

A fire in a barn killed our cat B.C., short for Barn Cat. I cried when I discovered he was dead. We found his body up against the rear door. He was such a friendly cat—he would bounce along the road to greet me as I walked to the barn. Not a morning goes by that I do not think of him. The barn has since been rebuilt, but it is not the same place without B.C.

I ached terribly when that little cat was killed.

If anyone were to ask me whether animals go to heaven, I wish I could say yes. I would like to think that they do. Can this vast universe be made just for us humans?

It is much easier for me to believe in a God who gives the gift of life to all living things, great and small, and if an animal fights for his or her life, I would like to think that a loving God will give that life back again.

Genesis 1:21

> So God created the great sea monsters
> and every living creature that moves, of
> every kind, with which the waters
> swarm, and every winged bird of every
> kind. And God saw that it was good.

KINDNESS

There are trillions of stars. Grains of sand on a beach are immeasurable. Such numbers are staggering. It is as if God went on overdrive, scattering all through creation an abundance—stars, sand, seeds, molecules, cells, and rays of light—beyond measure, at play in a moving and fecund universe.

Today is one day out of how many? Who can tell? It is just a day, like every other day, but this day that is before me is in need of kindness.

We look to the heavens for kindness. We walk the sands of our beaches, hoping for it. How wondrous that we can be kind.

Trillions of stars, trillions of grains. A single act of kindness is of more infinite value.

LUKE **6:38**

"Give, and it will be given to you. A good measure, pressed down, shaken together, running over, will be put into your lap; for the measure you give will be the measure you get back."

ALL SHOOK UP

I visited him every day in the hospital for several weeks. When he died early one morning his wife called me. She wanted me to ride with her to the hospital to pray with her before his body was removed from the room.

We sat near the bed. She held his still-warm hand and we prayed. She cried a bit, but she had been grieving for a long time, and now she was at peace with his death.

Suddenly a nurse's aid strolled into the room and in a cheery voice exclaimed, "Hi everybody" as she placed a large milk shake on the deceased's table, patted his head, told us that he looked good, and said to him, "Drink up. This shake is for you!" She smiled at us and then left the room.

His wife looked at me. I looked at her. And we both started to laugh. We prayed a bit more and said our good-byes. We left the milk shake on the table.

JOB 8:21

He will yet fill your mouth with
laughter,
and your lips with shouts of joy.

THE CAT LADY

She comes every night as the sun is setting. From where I sit in the woods, I can see her on the top of the hill. She is silhouetted behind the setting sun. Her clothes and hair shine with the brilliance of that dying light. She comes to feed the forest cats. She lightly hits a pan with a spoon as she tosses handfuls of the cat food onto the forest floor. The cats come from all directions with their tails raised high, almost perfectly straight. They are cautious. They move slowly toward her with hunger. But she has only good to give. She loves the cats, and she understands their ways. She has names for them all and watches for sick or missing ones. I have seen her search for an uncounted cat.

When I see the cat lady I think of God who comes to us only to do good, who seeks us out in ways we are hardly aware of. The features of God are hard to see, lost as they are in the brilliance of a light that is spread over all the world. Out of the light comes care and food, and names and searches. We approach to be fed and even cared for, and then we run back into the woods of our lives satisfied, only to return again out of our need for what God gives.

LUKE 11:11-12

"Is there anyone among you who, if your child asks for a fish, will give a snake instead of a fish? Or if the child asks for an egg, will give a scorpion?"

In Simple Black and White

Some things are enhanced to the extent that they do not distract. The less they startle, the more they convey.

For example, I like black and white photographs. Color photos distract me. The simple shades of black and white make it easier for me to reflect on the image.

Spirituality at its best should ease our hearts and eyes. Like a plain image in the center of a world of color, it should reveal the beauty that is all around us, a beauty that needs no distraction to reveal its true loveliness.

HABAKKUK 2:2

> Then the LORD answered me and said:
> Write the vision;
>> make it plain on tablets,
>> so that a runner may read it.

Help from Above

A little mouse got its head stuck in a hole in a metal drain in the middle of the floor in our bonsai barn at the monastery. It was helpless. Its little fanny was aimed at the heavens and wiggled furiously as the mouse tried to free itself from darkness and eventual doom. I never heard it sigh or groan in agony.

We tried everything we could think of to free the mouse but to no avail. The poor creature was frightened and seemed to go even deeper into the hole when we touched it.

Finally, a man who was helping us paint took a sponge and attached it firmly to the mousine buttocks and ever so gently rocked the mouse back and forth and slowly up. In a minute or so, the mouse emerged in one piece. The man carried the mouse, looking none the worse for its ordeal, outside and let it go.

At times life feels to me how that trap must have felt to that mouse. There are times I do not see a way out of the human predicament. Often our noses are in the wrong place and our rear ends facing the wrong way. But perhaps that is the only way God can grab us.

PSALM **40:2**

He drew me up from the desolate pit,
    out of the miry bog,
and set my feet upon a rock,
    making my steps secure.

A Bucket of Bees

I noticed the other day that there were bees around the top rim of a plastic bucket we've had in our barn for months. When I walked over for a closer look, I saw that they were making a large nest on the inside. I watched intently and kept my distance.

The hive in the making was covered with bees. Some were building while others were tending to the queen, whom I could not see. Others were depositing food in small cells, in which there were thousands of eggs that would survive through the colder months in a perfect dwelling. Come next spring the hive will come to new life as the tiny larvae mature and emerge as new bees. There will be a food supply waiting for them, left by the former colony.

Watching the bees work, it occurred to me that once the cold comes they will perish. Now they go selflessly about their work. It is a pure labor for life yet to come, life that is indeed from them but which they will never see.

I walked back to the monastery and prayed, "May I learn to be as selfless as those bees. May I learn to put others first and trust my place in a universal design not of my own making."

PSALM 119:36
___

> Turn my heart to your decrees,
> and not to selfish gain.

Rain Talk

I was once giving a homily when the clouds opened up and the rain burst down with a roar so loud that I stopped what I was saying. I waited and listened to the rain battering the roof. I could hear the rush of water running down the slates. The congregation was surrounded by a wall of wet and powerful sounds, all caused by the heavens unleashing millions of gallons of water.

It stopped as suddenly as it started. All that could then be heard were the drops falling from trees and gutters and the occasional splashes as a car drove through a puddle. I stood at the pulpit and thought about words and sentences; shards of grammar that try to speak of the things of God.

I smiled and looked around and told the small group gathered in the church that morning that for the first time it occurred to me that God has many languages and some are far better than what falls off the tongue. Whatever he had just said was trickling off the roof, dripping from the trees, and spraying from the wheels of a tire.

I sat down and let God finish the talk for that morning. It may have been the best homily I ever gave.

Deuteronomy 11:11

The land that you are crossing over to occupy is a land of hills and valleys, watered by rain from the sky.

THE MAGIC HOUSE

Mr. and Mrs. Wolke lived up the street from where my family lived when I was very young. Their house was small, like all the other houses on the street, but I remember it as a magic cottage that one might come across in an enchanted forest.

Mr. and Mrs. Wolke taught me how to make papier-mâché puppets with water and flour and newspaper and paint. Mrs. Wolke would then fashion costumes for my creations. I remember being especially proud of a pair of hillbilly puppets, a man and woman. Soon, there were other puppets, and other neighborhood kids and I made a small wooden theater from an orange crate and put on shows.

The Wolkes were Norwegian. At Christmas their tree was decorated with hundreds of ornaments from Norway. The tree sagged with the weight of its beauty. Mrs. Wolke gave us cookies and lemonade as we kids sat in front of the tree and looked at it with an awe and delight I remember to this day.

The best and most wondrous things in life, given with love, retain their magic.

SIRACH 40:16

> The reeds by any water or river bank
>   are plucked up before any grass;
> but kindness is like a garden of
>   blessings,
>   and almsgiving endures forever.

The Kiss

Linda was the first girl I ever kissed. It was like experiencing an entirely different world, one alive with wonder and desire, unlocked through strawberry flavored lipstick and a 1965 Chevrolet Impala.

Something eternal is involved with kissing. So it is that from a kiss can come weddings and babies and "till death do us parts."

I know that lips connect to the heart of another. And that is good. But as a monk (from *monos* meaning "alone"), I keep my lips to myself, knowing that such things lead where I cannot honestly go.

But I still feel love and passion. I feel them deeply and want to live from them.

So, I kiss with words. I love words and love others with words. I take them from my heart and put them on a page.

I kissed Linda and that was good and sweet. But I want to kiss the world, and God, and all I love, and all that is good, and I can't do that from a Chevy Impala.

Psalm 85:10

Steadfast love and faithfulness will meet;
righteousness and peace will kiss
each other

Irish Cowboy

His name was Desmond. We had lunch together in Ireland many years ago. He was a young boy brimming with questions about America. I sensed that he was leading up to something as he ate his chips, onto which he had poured a generous amount of vinegar.

He looked at me and his eyes widened, "Are there cowboys in America?" he asked

"Yes, there are," I calmly replied

"And is the sky golden where they are with miles and miles of plains under that sky?"

"Yes. Plains and sky as far as you can see."

He had read about such things, he told me, and had seen a lot of cowboy movies. I did not want to bring his dreams of America down to earth.

That was thirty years ago. I suspect Desmond's dreams have matured. I look back on that meal with him and remember his joy and wonder. I hope that God has blessed him with a life as full as the plains he so wanted to see and the freedom of the cowboy he aspired to be.

Sirach 34:20

> He lifts up the soul and makes the eyes sparkle;
> he gives health and life and blessing.

Learning to Ride

My first solo ride was on a tricycle that appeared beneath our Christmas tree in our house on Surrey Lane on a cold Christmas morning forty-five years ago. The trike was painted red and white, and red and white plastic ribbons flowed from the handlebars.

Those three wheels soon gave way to a more advanced vehicle, a green Schwinn bike that had training wheels attached to the rear spokes.

The day came when I wanted to learn to ride a bike with no training wheels.

I remember sitting on such a bike and clutching the handlebars as one of the bigger kids on the block ran along side of me, pushing the bike and then letting go. After several crashes, I did it. In an instant, I learned balance and was off. I must have ridden miles that day. It was a whole new life.

I think dying and being born again in Christ is something like that instant of learning balance on a bike. It is arrived at with love and encouragement. As simple as from here to there.

Psalm 90:10

The days of our life are seventy years,
    or perhaps eighty, if we are strong;
. . . they are soon gone, and we fly
        away.

THE CHOICE IS YOURS

She was despondent and crying about how her life was a mess. Her marriage was a hurtful one. Her self-esteem was shot.

We were sitting at her kitchen table, and she looked at me and said that she had thought of ending it all. Suicide, she said, looked attractive.

I did not know what to say, but I knew I had to say something. I asked her if she believed in an afterlife, and she told me that she did. Well, I said, if she did not like her situation in eternity surely she could not kill herself there. At least in her present situation she had more of a choice to work things out.

She looked at me and smiled and then we both started to laugh. "I never thought of it that way!" she replied.

That was a good number of years ago. From that day on, she took a good look at all the choices that were hers to make. The most important of them was simply the choice to make choices.

DEUTERONOMY **30:19**

Choose life so that you and your descendants may live.

Existential Truth

Lenore was a student of mine when I taught philosophy in the evenings to adults in a nearby college. She was in her late twenties and worked in an office during the day. On the first evening of class, I gave out the course requirements, which included a term paper to be handed in at the end of the course.

As the time to write the paper drew near, she approached me at the end of class and said that she did not know how to write on the existential philosophers we had covered. She simply froze when she tried to put her ideas into words.

We spoke for a long while that night. She told me a lot about her youth. She was one of ten children raised on a farm in Alabama. Her parents were poor but saved. All ten children were college graduates. She was the youngest. I told her to write about growing up, about her parents and whatever was warm enough to thaw her from the freeze she felt when she sat down to write.

She wrote an essay of power and beauty. It was the existential truth of her heart.

TOBIT 12:20

"So now get up from the ground, and acknowledge God. See, I am ascending to him who sent me. Write down all these things that have happened to you." And he ascended.

Unlikely Yield

He was a homeless man who had hit somewhere below bottom in Manhattan. He had become addicted to crack cocaine and lost nearly every stabilizing and good thing in his life.

He liked to write, however, and his words found their way into a newspaper that is written by and for street people. It is sold on the streets of Manhattan, and the monies are used to provide food and shelter for the homeless.

One day, a publisher was passing a trash can and spotted a discarded copy of the paper on top of the heap. Curious, he snatched it and began to read. The homeless man's writing impressed him. The publisher contacted the homeless man and eventually offered him a $200,000 advance for a book.

The once homeless man is doing well these days. He has been given a new lease on life and is drug-free, writing, and recovering much of what he had lost.

I like the idea that words tossed away into a trash bin grew into an undreamed-of harvest.

Psalm 113:7

> He raises the poor from the dust,
>   and lifts the needy from the ash
> heap.

WHAT DESPAIR HOPES FOR

One night a writer told me that on a trip to Africa, where he had seen so much human suffering, he questioned many things that he had long taken for granted. Not least of these was the existence of a benevolent and redemptive God. He had reached a point where he saw no reason for ultimate hope. He thought it honest to take despair as a more truthful way of describing life. "For me, hope doesn't really exist," he concluded.

He told me that he wanted to write about his loss of hope and the cleansing nature of despair. He explained that only through the eyes of despair can we see things as they really are.

I told him that if it meant that much to him, he should go ahead and write about it. He asked me if I thought there would be people interested in such a bleak view of things. "Yes," I said, "despair hopes for the company of others."

PSALM **119:116**

Uphold me according to your promise,
that I may live,
and let me not be put to shame
in my hope.

THE AIRPORT

Many years ago, Mom and I went to the New Orleans airport to meet my brother Peter. He was flying in from Los Angeles. At first the flight was delayed for an hour. Then the delay was extended to two hours. We ended up spending the entire day waiting for him in that busy airport.

We made the most of it. It was pleasurable and peaceful waiting with each other.

I mentioned the experience to my mother a few days ago, and she startled me when she said with vivid recollection, "Remember the young Scotsman who wore the beautiful heavy coat in such a hot place and how friendly he was?" I vaguely remembered him.

Memory is best when shared. The past offers more of itself when recalled by two or more.

PSALM 77:11

I will call to mind the deeds of the
LORD;
I will remember your wonders of
old.

The Best Laid Plans

I told a friend that I was worried about the outcome of a project. I had barely started, and already I wanted to control the outcome.

She listened patiently and suggested that come spring I grow a garden. Plant the seeds, she said, and care for them every day. Grow things that have no other use than their beauty, like flowers. Watch them as they rise from the earth, admire them, and learn from them when they die. Then cover the earth, she said, and promise to do it again the following spring.

Though my flower garden never came to be, my friend taught me that everything—project or garden included—has a right to its own way of becoming, and the best I can do is help it along by working on it bit by bit and then letting it go.

PROVERBS **19:20-21**

Listen to advice and accept instruction,
that you may gain wisdom for the
future.
The human mind may devise many
plans,
but it is the purpose of the LORD
that will be established.

Foundations in Theology

Right next to where I sit in the woods there is a large piece of pillar-shaped concrete left over from when our church was built by the monks many years ago.

Every square inch of our beautiful church came from the monks' love and labor. Its beauty had something to do with drawing me to this particular monastery.

The monks before me constructed the church during the convening of the Second Vatican Council in the 1960s. The time was one of wonder and genuine awe, but the monks had little time to keep up with what was going on at the Council.

There are times when I catch myself faulting the older monks for not being up to date in their theology. Should they have read more?

How foolish of me. I sit in their theology every day. It is a theology so abundant that there are pieces to spare.

Ephesians **2:21**

> In Christ Jesus the whole structure is
> joined together and grows into a temple
> in the Lord.

High Drama

A hush fell over the theater as the house lights dimmed and the curtain was about to rise. In the seats that night was a chic Manhattan crowd, finely dressed and coifed for an evening of dinner and drama. The couple in front of me had been whispering softly to each other during those last few minutes before the rising of the curtain. They seemed so in love and happy to be there with each other.

The play began. Just moments after the first few lines were spoken from the stage, the beam of a small flashlight shone on the couple. The usher leaned over to them, with tickets in her hand, aimed the light at the tickets and said to the couple, "I'm afraid that you are in the wrong seats." The man shifted uncomfortably and retrieved his ticket stub and gave it to the usher, who quickly looked at it and said, "These are for next week." The woman glared at her husband and then called him an obscene name. Everyone around them heard the words. Pity for him filled the air. The couple rose and left with the usher. The new arrivals sat in their seats as if settling into a vacated coffin.

The sad couple's performance wasn't worth the price of admission.

PSALM 37:8

Refrain from anger, and forsake wrath.
Do not fret—it leads only to evil.

Woman of Sorrow

For many weeks now a woman comes daily to our monastery church to pray and chant the psalms. She sits in the far back, where there is less light but a better atmosphere for solitude. She is very pretty, with long black hair and is always simply dressed. I wondered about her, and one of the monks finally told me that she recently lost her son, a teenager, and that a friend of hers told her to come to the church and pray.

I now see the sorrow and understand her distance. But I also see peace and more than a trace of serenity on her face. I hope she is finding them in her heart, as well. Peace and serenity we have in ample supply at the monastery. I am grateful to be part of the space that she needs to heal and carry her pain with such dignity and courage.

Matthew 5:4

> "Blessed are those who mourn, for they will be comforted."

MOUNDS OF WISDOM

Earlier today as I was walking, I took particular notice of the ant mounds in the woods around the monastery. Some of them are much larger than basketballs. I observed hundreds of diligent ants making the finishing touches on these marvels of natural engineering. The mounds will provide protection from the harshness of winter and serve as storehouses for the next generation's food.

As they did in previous ages, arguments for the existence of a God or higher intelligences abound today. Through the many winters over all the earth, ants have exhibited a wisdom surely not of their own making. Their ways of being speak volumes on the existence of a wise and caring creator.

PROVERBS 24:3

By wisdom a house is built,
    and by understanding it is established.

God's Web

I spent a long and enjoyable afternoon in the woods surrounding the monastery reading Doris Grumbach's *The Presence of Absence,* a beautiful book about her lifelong search for God. She had an experience of God many years ago and has been seeking to recapture the feeling ever since.

My eyes grew tired, and I got up to walk back home. I had my head bowed, knowing well the path that stretched ahead of me. I walked right into a spider's silver thread and felt its tight stickiness on my head. I stepped back and saw the large and beautiful web, glistening and waving back and forth from the slight collision. The spider scrambled to and fro, perhaps thinking it had trapped some delicacy. I ducked beneath the thread and walked on.

God's love is like that spider's web, strung all through the earth, catching us every now and then. Shining strands of kindness, beauty, hope, joy, and divine comfort weave in and out of our lives ensnaring us when we least expect it.

Wisdom 9:16

> We can hardly guess at what is on
> earth,
> and what is at hand we find with labor;
> but who has traced out what is in the
> heavens?

Put Some Distance between You

The poet Kimiko Hahn said in an interview that she needs to leave a place in order to write about it. Distance affords her a deeper and more emotional grasp of whom or what she loves there.

How true it is that our love grows with distance. Places or persons become more vivid when we stand back from them. We see them for what they really are . . . and what they always were.

JOHN **16:7**

"Nevertheless I tell you the truth: it is to your advantage that I go away, for if I do not go away, the Advocate will not come to you; but if I go, I will send him to you."

THE DOORS

I once went to an art exhibit in the Soho district of Manhattan displaying the work of a woman who painted stunning portraits on unusual wooden doors. There were doors of all shapes and sizes. The artist had collected them from construction sites, dumps, and abandoned buildings and houses.

Since I visited that gallery I have come across many a discarded door. The doors seem to wait to be discovered by someone who recognizes their potential and genuine worth. With vision, paint, and care, they could be transformed into portals that open one's eyes and heart to beauty. Seeds to trees to doors to galleries to portraits: all beautiful in their unique ways, all awaiting to become something ever more wondrous.

REVELATION 21:5

And the one who was seated on the throne said, "See, I am making all things new."

THE WHOLE TRUTH

Bobby had a statue of the Madonna in his hands. The bottom was broken and he had the pieces on the small desk in his room. He asked whether I could fix it.

I came back to the cloister and found some glue. As I was leaving the office, I saw a small bottle of White Out. The color looked to be a perfect match for the statue.

I found Bobby, and it took just a few minutes to put the pieces together with the glue. Once the glue hardened, I covered the seams with the White Out. Bobby took the statue and held it in his arms and smiled. "Good as new," he said.

Bobby is confined to a wheelchair. His arms and legs are twisted. I am sure that many prayers have been said for his body to be whole. But healing comes in stages, and God has already made Bobby's heart as good as new.

JEREMIAH **33:6**

I am going to bring it recovery and healing; I will heal them and reveal to them abundance of prosperity and security.

LIKE UNTO GOD

The classic definition of God is a Being who was, is, and ever shall be all knowing, all powerful, all just, all happy, all self-contained. How humans have longed to be the same.

But do Christians not say that to take up a cross is to take up the very life of God? If so, then is not the living God one who is sorrow as well as joy, weakness as well as strength? The experiences of the human heart are like unto God.

ROMANS 8:16-17

We are children of God, and if children, then heirs, heirs of God and joint heirs with Christ—if, in fact, we suffer with him so that we may also be glorified with him.

COMPANY

I was, I thought, alone in the barn, wrapping bonsai pots for shipment. The large doors were open.

I looked up and saw a dog I had never seen before, sitting looking right at me with his tongue hanging out of his mouth. The pooch looked happy to be recognized. I whistled and he approached just a few feet and then stopped, sat back down, and stayed for the two hours that I worked. I tried to approach him, but the little guy shied away. I found in myself a growing sense of pleasure in this doggie-polite way of being in the world.

When I returned in the afternoon my visitor was gone. Later I found out that a little girl had called the monastery office asking if anyone had seen her dog on the property. Her father drove her over to pick up the dog.

The world was a happier place that night: happy dog, happy little girl, and happy me for the unexpected company that day.

PSALM 21:6

You bestow on him blessings forever;
you make him glad with the joy
of your presence.

BYGONES

My seventh grade teacher, a young nun, used to call our class Disciples of Satan and Instruments of the Devil. Although I didn't understand it at the time, I later realized that she was not a very happy person when she taught us in grammar school, and admittedly we kids did very little to inspire her to think of us as the children of the gospels whom Jesus so loved.

Many years after I was ordained, I heard that she was in a nearby hospital. Her condition was serious, and she was in a lot of pain. When I stopped in for a visit, she was pleased to see me. She appeared lighthearted and was proud of what I had become.

Before I left, she asked for my blessing. I smiled and asked whether I should beseech the powers of light or darkness. She remembered her long-ago name-calling and laughed. She sweetly requested a kiss good-bye.

SIRACH **28:6**

Remember the end of your life and set enmity aside.

Give It Up

We humans have a great need to gratify our senses. Each day we want our eyes, ears, noses, tongues, and hands to take in all that they can. We are in constant danger of sensory overload. The best way I know to observe the upcoming Lenten season is to deprive the senses of stimulation and offer my mind and heart to a higher power.

Daniel 9:3

Then I turned to the Lord God, to seek an answer by prayer and supplication with fasting and sackcloth and ashes.

Hoss

Hoss—part pit bull, part boxer—arrived in a truck with his owner, Mike, and sat on the front seat while Mike went through our bonsai barn selecting pots. I greeted Hoss, and he lavished my hand with slurps.

I went back to my work area and wrapped pots. Hoss soon jumped from the van to look for Mike. He sniffed, bounded from one object to another, sniffed again, wagged his tail. Mike called and Hoss leaped toward him. More licks, more jumping up and down with an abandon only dogs exhibit so well.

For Hoss, a leap from a truck window opened a whole new and exciting world. What a grace it would be to seize each day with such delight.

LUKE **6:23**

"Rejoice in that day and leap for joy, for surely your reward is great in heaven."

The Cake That Fed a Multitude

After a fire in our bonsai barn destroyed much of our business equipment, Karen (a laywoman who runs the wholesale end of the business) switched our e-mail address to her home in Atlanta. When I had to send and receive e-mail, I did so through Karen.

One morning I was reading behind the barn when Karen walked up with a smile on her face and said, "Well, you have a publisher!" She handed me an e-mail from Chicago confirming that a contract was being drawn up for my first book. I was thrilled to actual tears, and she gave me a hug.

We went into the barn office and there neatly laid out was a cake, freshly brewed coffee, napkins and forks for a celebration with my fellow workers.

I wanted the whole world in that room. There was enough kindness and generosity that morning to feed a multitude.

PSALM 63:5

My soul is satisfied as with a rich feast,
and my mouth praises you
with joyful lips.

Enlightenment

A fellow student was in the throes of writing a dissertation on the concept of Nirvana; thus she was researching the ineffable, the beyond words, the never-to-be-grasped. I asked her how she could write about the unwriteable? How does one footnote the unfootnotable? Maybe, I suggested, she could simply hand in blank pages to prove that she attained the unknowable, the academically undoable.

She looked at me with contempt and retorted, "You don't understand Nirvana." She picked up her books and left in a huff.

Maybe I should have admitted to the woman that I don't buy the concept of Nirvana. When I die, I want enlightenment to come in words. I want to hear my name called by a God who loves me. "Hey, Jeff" will do nicely.

Isaiah 45:3

> I will give you the treasures of darkness
> and riches hidden in secret places,
> so that you may know that it is I, the
> Lord,
> the God of Israel, who call you
> by your name.

Fixing to Storm

Mr. Connolly was the grandfather of my childhood friend John. He visited from North Dakota every year. We lived in New Jersey, so North Dakota sounded far away and exotic.

One blustery November day, the neighborhood kids were at John's house when the skies started to look ominous. It was turning gray, and there was that special feel of snow in the air. As the first flakes began to fall, Mr. Connolly narrowed his eyes and stated with confidence, "It's goin' to be a whopper." Within hours the howling wind brought with it a blizzard that lasted two days and broke many a record for snowfall in the Northeast.

It amazed us that Mr. Connolly had predicted as much from just a few preliminary flakes.

When a thoughtless word, an unkind gesture, or a mean-spirited remark brings a storm of pain in its wake, I often wish I had Mr. Connolly's knack for reading the early weather signs.

Mark 16:20

They went out and proclaimed
the good news everywhere, while the Lord
worked with them and confirmed the
message by the signs that accompanied it.

Eucharist

A tribe in the Amazon, hidden from civilization for years, was filmed by a documentary crew and eventually their story was told on American television. The encroachment of the Western World quickly took its toll on these people.

The tribe had no natural antibodies to fight off diseases to which much of the rest of the world's population had become immune. A young woman in the tribe died from a disease she had contracted from this new world contamination. The tribespeople cried and wailed at her death.

Fearing that she would be lonely in the afterworld, the tribespeople stored her lifeless body until it decayed to the bones. These were then taken, mashed into a fine powder, and mixed into a soup. The family and friends sat in a circle and with longing and reverence passed the soup bowl around as each one drank from it. In this way they were able to take her spirit into themselves and were heartened that she would never suffer from loneliness.

John 6:56

> "Those who eat my flesh and drink my blood abide in me, and I in them. Just as the living Father sent me, and I live because of the Father, so whoever eats me will live because of me."

BROADSIDE COLLISION

My mom never liked driving a car, but with seven kids she had little choice.

One day she was driving down our street and out of the corner of her eye saw a little boy dart from between two parked cars on his tricycle. She did not have time to stop, and he drove right into the side of the car. Mom pulled over and burst into tears. She remained in the car, frozen in her fear and afraid to get out of the car and go to the injured boy. Soon there was a knock at the window and through her tears she recognized a neighbor. She lowered the window and begged the man to look near the car for the boy. He did. There was no boy, he told her. And no bike. The kid had bounced off the car, righted his bike, and went along his merry way.

Most things that hit us broadside startle us, but they tend to bounce off and move on.

JOSHUA **1:9**

"Be strong and courageous; do not be frightened or dismayed, for the LORD your God is with you wherever you go."

Star Bursts

Through the open kitchen window I could hear my mom whisper as she was putting away the dishes, "I love you. I love you." My dad had just passed away, and I was standing outside the house staring at the stars.

I read a theory that we come from the stars. Long ago, great bursts of energy from exploding stars evolved into life. The stuff of stars thus became the raw material of our mourning and loss.

Those stars were far away that night, and as I heard my mother's plaintive cries, I wished that the stars would whisper back in that particular voice she loved so much.

Baruch 3:34

The stars shone in their watches, and
were glad;
he called them, and they said, "Here
we are!"
They shone with gladness for him
who made them.

ART APPRECIATION

For poet Elizabeth Bishop, some poems took years to write. Bob Dylan, on the other hand, claims he wrote "The Gates of Eden" while sitting in a car in a motel parking lot.

Capturing life on paper or canvas or stone may take hours or years. But to appreciate such art takes but a second or two. To have a taste for it, an eye for it, an ear for it, a heart for it, is to be blessed.

WISDOM **6:10**

For they will be made holy who observe
holy things in holiness.

Valentine's Day

Years ago, on China's Great Wall, I saw initials and hearts and arrows—the marks of lovers, some of which were centuries old. The carvings were in many languages, but their messages were much the same. I suppose that we write on monuments to attest to the lasting nature of our loves. How great is the memorial where God's love for us is writ large?

Hebrews 13:14

For here we have no lasting city, but we are looking for the city that is to come.

CAKEY BUILDUP

There was enough dessert for all the kids, but one boy did not want the other kids to have any. So he ate nearly the whole cake. Then he got sick and threw up. The other kids cried and moaned when they realized that there was no more cake. But they were glad that the greedy boy got sick.

His mother was distressed when she saw her son heave and heave. She was happy when he said that he felt better. Suddenly, another cake was brought up from the basement refrigerator, and all the kids were happy that there was more cake. Each had a fair share.

The boy's mother felt sorry that he got sick, so she gave him a piece of the new cake. He said that he felt better and ate it. And then she gave him another. And he ate that, too. The other kids glared at him with disgust. He smiled at them. The mother was happy that he was well again.

I still hear that story from the kids who were there that day. They have their own kids now, and I doubt that there are any extra cakes held in reserve.

SIRACH **37:29**

Do not be greedy for every delicacy,
　and do not eat without restraint.

OPEN WIDE

"Is this all you do?" I innocently asked the dental technician as she was preparing to clean my teeth. I meant it as a way of expressing a sincere interest in her periodontic extracurriculars. But I stressed the wrong words in the question, and she took it as an insult. Then she attacked. I could not say a thing because my mouth was open. I suffered in silence.

She prodded and poked and picked and flossed and scraped and polished and then repeated the steps with vigor and vengeance. She used her tools of pain well.

Now I only go to Tootsie. She is a soft flosser. We talk deep things, but never once have I asked her what else is on her periodontic agenda.

JOB 33:7
_____

No fear of me need terrify you;
　　my pressure will not be heavy on you.

Mrs. Arntz's Magic House

My mom recently told me that Mrs. Arntz sold her house in our old neighborhood. She is the last neighbor I knew still living there.

As kids, we had a lot of fun at Mrs. Arntz's house, especially in the loft above her large garage. In the fifth or sixth grade, we had sleepovers with her children. We would sneak out at night and walk the streets, feeling that we were committing the worst of evils. Some years later, a group of us formed a band and practiced in the Arntz basement. I can still see Johnny Arntz banging away at the piano—his left foot sliding and stomping to the beat, his right foot tending the pedals. A huge mound of Newport cigarette butts sat in an old ash tray on top of the piano.

I will write to Mrs. Arntz today and thank her for what she need not and cannot pack away: the love I have for those times she and her family gave to me. Those were magic years. They still work their magic on me.

Nehemiah 12:46

For in the days of David and Asaph long ago there was a leader of the singers, and there were songs of praise and thanksgiving to God.

DIFFERENT LOVES

A friend of mine reared seven children, and over the years I have often been amazed at how different each is from the other. It is hard to believe that they grew up in the same house. One is shy, another extroverted. One is overly sensitive, another quite gruff. Yet each shines in his or her own way. My friend once told me with pride, "I love them each in a different way, but just as deeply."

I think of her when I ponder the differences in people. Each of us has different needs, different temperaments, different life experiences. Perhaps God, too, loves each of us equally but uniquely, according to the wondrous variations that exist among so many sons and daughters.

ROMANS **12:6-8**

> We have gifts that differ according to the grace given to us; prophecy, in proportion to faith; ministry, in ministering; the teacher, in teaching; the exhorter, in exhortation; the giver, in generosity; the leader, in diligence; the compassionate, in cheerfulness.

Heart's Desire

I met a woman at a party many years ago, and later told her how pretty I thought she was that night. We became friends. She lives far away now, and I miss her. I recently asked whether she thought much about the past, and she said she does when she takes walks at night beneath the stars.

I think of my friend walking beneath the stars, beauty beneath beauty, and how her loveliness, like the stars, is far away from me now.

I wish my friend well and pray that I may be patient with my seeking heart until the Lord gives all of us a life that has no distance, no past, no vastness save for that of our heart's true desire.

Psalm 132:13-14

For the Lord has chosen Zion;
> he has desired it for his habitation:
"This is my resting place forever;
> here I will reside, for I have desired
>> it."

Bells

The big bell in our bell tower at the monastery tolls every morning at four sharp.

When that first gong sounds, without fail, the geese down by the lake make an incredible racket.

Geese must not have much of a memory. You would think that by now they would expect the bell's morning clang and not make such fuss.

But I am not without the same short memory. Only recently have I begun to notice how I react to certain situations and am trying to learn what bells in my environment send me squawking when I should just let them ring.

Deuteronomy 27:15

And all the people shall respond, saying, "Amen!"

A Funny Thing Happened

The cultural anthropologist Mary Douglas wrote of a missionary who was teaching young African children the parable of Dives and Lazarus. The children listened intently and then, much to the consternation of the missionary, broke out into a roar of laughter at the key point of tale. It was some time later that the baffled missionary came to understand that the children were identifying the Christian God as their trickster god Ifa—a laughing, frivolous divinity—who, in the character of Abraham, was being so harsh on the rich man in the parable.

It is difficult for me to imagine a God who laughs, who appreciates irony, who may even play tricks on us. Yet we are of God's likeness, and certainly each of us, like those African students, appreciates a good joke.

Acts **13:52**

And the disciples were filled with joy and with the Holy Spirit.

IMMEDIATE GRATIFICATION

The publisher of my first book called me out of the blue to say that the newly published book had arrived from the printer and that he was mailing me several copies overnight. I felt a flood of joy, and only later did it dawn on me how happy he was, too. This man knew how eager I was to see the fruits of my labor, and he extended himself to ensure a fast delivery of the book. My joy became his joy.

I learned a lasting lesson that day.

Joy comes to us all in many guises, and one of the best of them is sharing the joy of another.

1 JOHN 1:4

We are writing these things so that our joy may be complete.

GROPING FOR GOD

A friend recently wrote to me that he was worried that he had lost the sense of God in his life. He remembered earlier times when simple things like walking his dog along the shore of a lake offered him an experience of God's presence.

I knew my friend had recently married and had been busy with the responsibilities of a new shared life. He was, he wrote, very happy that he married.

I do not think my friend has lost touch with God at all. Perhaps it is just that his experience of God is maturing before he has been given the words to deal with it.

Experience precedes language. Wonder and joy come first, and it may take a long while for us to look back and see that God was always there. God never abandons us, and God's presence in every aspect of our lives should give us courage to look forward to tomorrow.

ACTS 17:26-27

From one ancestor he made all nations to inhabit the whole earth, and he allotted the times of their existence and the boundaries of the places where they would live, so that they would search for God and perhaps grope for him and find him— though indeed he is not far from each one of us.

God Talk

Linda was my German professor in graduate school. The course lasted only eight weeks, and in that time she taught us enough German to translate theological and philosophical German into English. I still remember much of the language and use it whenever possible.

Like other teachers who made a lasting impression on me, the secret of Linda's charm was that she loved teaching and the subject she taught. She had mastered the German language and along the way had developed a real heart for people. A happy person, she made the journey into the complexities of German a delight.

In the end, Linda taught me much more than the German language; she taught me the language of life, which is what God speaks.

PSALM 35:28

Then my tongue shall tell of your
righteousness
and of your praise all day long.

WHEN TOMORROW NEVER COMES

In the beautiful book *The Eternal Now*, theologian
Paul Tillich portrays the Christian God as one who
creates life in new and lovingly wondrous ways each
and every second. God's love sustains all moments.
The eternal spills into the now from whence all time
comes.

There is an Amazonian tribe of people who have no
word for *later*, *tomorrow*, *next*, and the like. Their
lives and interests are so totally absorbed by the
present that the future has no reference for them.
They live from moment to moment.

"For those who love, time is not," says Tillich.

MATTHEW **6:34**

"Do not worry about tomorrow, for
tomorrow will bring worries of its own.
Today's trouble is enough for today."

Hyperlinks

It amazes me that with the press of a few buttons on my computer I can insert a link that will automatically transport me from one text to another, from one web site to another, even from one country to another. I can make links to people all over the world in seconds.

But all the while I am here, in a room in a Trappist monastery in Georgia on a cloudy day.

I hope my words, written in silence, help link those who hear or read them to the living God who has linked us all together.

Isaiah **50:4**

> The LORD God has given me
>   the tongue of a teacher,
> that I may know how to sustain
>   the weary with a word.
> Morning by morning he wakens—
>   wakens my ear
>   to listen as those who are taught.

Making Room

My first-grade teacher told us to always leave room on our chairs for our guardian angels.

This may seem a childish lesson, but the wisdom of making room for the unseen has been something I have struggled to take to heart my entire life. I do not think it is possible to trust life without leaving ample room for what cannot be touched or seen or measured.

It was easy enough to move a few inches on a long-ago school bench and leave room for a spirit. Only later did I realize how hard it is to make room in my life for the only Presence that really matters.

Psalm 77:19

Your way was through the sea,
　　your path, through the mighty
　　　　waters;
　　yet your footprints were unseen.

THE SILENCE OF BEAUTY

While taking a walk on the monastery grounds, I saw a single flower—a bright yellow one—just starting its life in a bloom by the side of the road. Surrounded by dirt, some wisps of grass and weeds, and an anthill, its solitary beauty was pronounced.

Flowers, of course, say nothing. They spin not a word. Their only labor is to be what they are.

They are worth of emulation.

LUKE **12:27**

> "Consider the lilies, how they grow:
> they neither toil nor spin; yet I tell you,
> even Solomon in all his glory was not
> clothed like one of these."

DELIA

Delia was a simple, good, and loving woman. Yet when she died, she left behind nothing that could be highlighted in her obituary except the list of those who survived her.

She was widowed early in her marriage and raised five children well. She worked cleaning houses and attended Mass as often as she could. She had few possessions and more often than not gave away what little she had. She loved to see others happy, took to heart their troubles, and wove their joys and sorrows into her own prayers.

She learned to love in the most ordinary ways amid the most ordinary of circumstances. What an extraordinary life!

1 CORINTHIANS 13:4-7

Love is patient; love is kind; love is not envious or boastful or arrogant or rude. It does not insist on its own way; it is not irritable or resentful; it does not rejoice in wrongdoing, but rejoices in the truth. It bears all things, believes all things, hopes all things, endures all things.

A Parting Gift

I visited a man in his home almost daily for several months as he lay dying from lung cancer. Disease had ravaged him—his body had wasted away to barely more than a frame. He was a heavy smoker, and his disease did not stop him from enjoying a cigarette or two right up to a few days before he passed away.

He never married and lived with his brother and sister-in-law, whom I got to know quite well over the course of my visits. When the man passed away, I was called to the house to say some prayers.

When it was time to go, the brother reached into his wallet to give me a few dollars. "Buy something for yourself," he said. I thanked him but declined. "Well, we want to give you something," he insisted. He turned around and reached on top of the refrigerator for a carton of his dead brother's cigarettes. "He would have wanted you to have these. It is the least we can do."

I took the carton. I smoked the cigarettes.

It was the least I could do.

Romans **11:35**

"Who has given a gift to him,
to receive a gift in return?"

To Those Who Wait

One time, I forgot I was to pick up a friend. When I finally remembered, I was not near a phone, so I couldn't call him to say I'd be late.

When I pulled in front of his house, he was waiting on the porch. I thought he would be angry. But when I approached him, he smiled and said that he knew I had probably forgotten. He had been reading a book, he said, and enjoyed the wait. He knew that I would come eventually.

Life is a wait for God. To wait patiently is to know that our Savior will come. To wait wisely is to use our time well. To wait lovingly is to joyfully embrace the gifts that lie before us.

LAMENTATIONS **3:25-26**

The LORD is good to those who wait for
him,
to the soul that seeks him.
It is good that one should wait quietly
for the salvation of the LORD.

Narrow Passage

The Wellmont was a large movie theater in my hometown. There was a door from the balcony to a fire escape that led down to an alley. One of us kids would buy a ticket, run upstairs, and stuff a shoe into the fire escape door just a narrow crack to hold it open without letting light pour into the theater to give us away. When the theater darkened and the movie began, the rest of us ran up the stairs, through the door, and into the theater balcony for free movies. We never got caught. Every Saturday a magical world that took us far from New Jersey awaited us through that narrow opening.

To enter Paradise may not be as easy as sneaking into the Wellmont. But, it would not surprise me if Mary or Joseph or even Peter himself has wedged a shoe in a pearly gate on the backside of heaven. I'll bet God may even smile and look the other way.

Luke 13:24

"Strive to enter through the narrow door; for many, I tell you, will try to enter and will not be able."

"Saved!"

The one television my family owned when I was growing up was on the back porch of our house. It was surrounded by a hodgepodge of chairs and one long, green, musty-smelling couch.

If one of the kids had to answer the phone, go to the bathroom, answer the door, or grab a snack, he or she had to yell, "Saved!" If this was done, the person was supposed to get the seat back; if no save were called, the person was out of luck. This ritual, however, became more nuanced as time went on: a seat could be saved for so many minutes, through the next commercial, etc. "Special Saves" involved asking a sister or brother to actually keep a hand on the seat in the occupant's absence. There were, of course, fights galore when these various saves were unrecognized or denied.

Not long ago, while we were watching a movie here at the monastery (which doesn't happen too often), an elderly monk got up from the seat next to me and whispered, "Saved," while pointing to his chair. Then he ambled off to the bathroom.

"Is this a commercial save or a two-minute special?" I wondered as he left the room.

Esther 14:14

"Save us by your hand, and help me, who am alone and have no helper but you, O Lord."

The Voice of the Sea

I have often seen solitary figures standing on a peaceful shoreline quietly peering out to the sea as if listening to what the waters whisper to them. The gentle surf can calm a troubled soul.

But the sea swells and rages as well. What is it saying to us then?

Perhaps it is wise to hearken equally to the message of those ferocious storms—much like the squalls that batter our hearts and drown our emotions. Our souls grow strong in both tranquility and trial.

Matthew 14:25

Early in the morning he came walking toward them on the sea.

THE POWER OF WORDS

My old friend paced the room, telling me that he wanted to write a letter to a person who had hurt him. He had composed the letter over and over in his head but was too angry to write it. He knew that the words would be harsh.

My friend is of good heart. Should he eventually sit and write that letter, I have a feeling that his heart will win over his head. Words have a way of wresting from us the best that we are. They offer associations of memory, places, and affection. They turn the soil of our minds and expose treasures beneath the surface.

REVELATION **21:5**

"Write this, for these words are trustworthy and true."

EMPTY TRUNKS

I went to Europe for an extended stay with a trunkful of my beloved books. I lugged that trunk through train stations across the continent, but I stubbornly refused to rid myself of the burden. When I finally settled in Geneva, I read only two or three of the books. I left the rest there with my sister and returned to the States a much wiser and more carefree traveler.

Now I make a regular habit of checking what other baggage I lug around in the recesses of my mind that keeps me from traveling lightly.

LUKE **9:3**

> "Take nothing for your journey, no staff, nor bag, nor bread, nor money–not even an extra tunic."

The Death of a Writer

One of the monks told me today that the brilliant writer Andre Dubus had died of a fatal heart attack. A sadness overcame me. I had met him only once, and we corresponded a little over the years. His description of people and their heartaches and joy was nothing short of sublime. He helped me see more deeply and lovingly into human life. And now he is gone and will write no more.

But he left behind his words, his stories and essays. And I will reread them and they will touch my heart again and again. Words have that kind of power.

They are a resurrection of sorts. Andre Dubus' words will continue to rise from the page and call people to share in a life he now lives to the fullest.

Jᴏʜɴ **8:51**

"Very truly, I tell you, whoever keeps my word will never see death."

THE BIRTH OF A WRITER

One of the monks was struggling to write. Draft after draft flowed from his pen, but he was unable to move beyond a few pages.

I had just read *Bird by Bird*, Anne Lamott's wonderful book on creativity and writing. On a whim, I checked for her name in the phone book, called her, introduced myself, and explained the situation.

Three days later a signed copy of *Bird by Bird* arrived at the monastery. On the inside cover Ms. Lamott had written the warmest words of encouragement to my friend. Two months later, his first finished story won an award and much needed recognition from a local writer's group.

My friend is still writing. May Anne Lamott be blessed for her act of kindness that bore such wondrous and tangible fruit. She helped create a writer.

JAMES 1:17

Every generous act of giving, with every perfect gift, is from above, coming down from the Father of lights, with whom there is no variation or shadow due to change.

HOLY PLACE

I often write behind an old barn on the monastery grounds. The large doors are long gone, and I place a chair right inside where the doors once were. Rain or shine, I find this spot perfectly suited to my needs.

The barn, without a doubt, has seen better days. Vines ramble up and down the walls and in and out of the windows. The wood is bare. The barn is filled with an odd collection of unwanted items: discarded pieces of furniture, old doors, plumbing fixtures, piles of wood and marble. Birds fly in and out at will.

I love the place. It seems to have evolved to its present state in an organic way.

I hope that when I am old I will like what has been gathered in me over the years.

PSALM 24:3-4

Who shall ascend the hill of the LORD?
  And who shall stand in his holy place?
Those who have clean hands and pure
    hearts,
    who do not lift up their souls to what is
    false

Going Places

Catholic Worker founder Dorothy Day believed
that prayers could move God to change the past.

In the stillness of my cloistered life, my mind is
free to roam. Often I will let my mind's eye wander
about the rooms of the house in which I grew up.
Detail after detail emerges: colors of drapes, dish
rags hanging on the porcelain sink, location of
light switches, lion's feet on the bathtub, views
from windows, little statues Mom had in different
rooms. I can see my whole family, too, and recall
how they looked, how their voices sounded, even
specific pieces of clothing they wore.

God was there, too, in the rooms, behind the
drapes, at the table—moving among us and loving
us.

I wonder if the past is still somehow alive in God?
I pray that God watch over us, guide us, and
change our pasts into a brighter future.

Mark 10:27

Jesus looked at them and said, "For
mortals it is impossible, but not for God;
for God all things are possible."

May I Call You Friend?

I have been blessed throughout my life with many friends. Friendship has come as a gift. The deep and lasting ties I now enjoy came to my life through no design or calculation on my part.

With the love I encounter in each friendship, I feel my friendship with God strengthened. I pray to find in God a friend. But, as with any friendship, I know I can not force it or plan it. It comes as pure gift.

Isaiah **41:8-9**

You, Israel, my servant,
      Jacob, whom I have chosen,
      the offspring of Abraham, my friend;
you whom I took from the ends of the
         earth.
      and called from it's farthest corners,
saying to you, "You are my servant,
      I have chosen you and not cast you
         off."

CROSS CULTURES

Cultures are universes unto themselves: French culture; Amazon culture; sixteenth-century culture; rock 'n' roll culture; pop culture; high culture; low culture. Each is a collection of human strivings, successes, failures, joys, desires.

Monastic culture is no holier than any of the above. Perhaps it is a bit more concentrated, a bit more rarified—a place from which to see the goodness in the many cultural expressions of humans and to be grateful for the God who makes such beauty through them all.

WISDOM 1:14

For he created all things so that they
    might exist;
the generative forces of the world are
    wholesome,
and there is no destructive poison in
    them,
and the dominion of Hades is not on
    earth.

MEMORIES OF GRANDMA

I found a tiny metal box in an old drawer here at the monastery. It once contained suppositories for hemorrhoids. I turned the box over and on the side was printed "Store in a cool place." For a moment I was confused: store what, where?

My grandmother used to tell my siblings and me not to sit on a cold curb in the winter because we would "catch colds in our fannies." I thought about her advice when I read the injunction on the little box.

My memories of Grandma are stored in a warm place—in my heart—never to grow cold...no matter where I sit.

PROVERBS 22:6

Train children in the right way,
and when old, they will not stray.

Forget Your Worries

I took a walk around the monastery on a gorgeous sunny day graced with a cool and constant
breeze. I set out absorbed with worry, but then I
passed a large budding tree and noticed tiny
flowers sprouting near its trunk. The birds were
particularly active that day, flitting here and there
to gather what they needed to build their nests.
The ground was moist from rain that had fallen
during the night, and the grass was a luscious
green. So amazed was I with all these living
things coming to life, called to newness by a
divine process that summons them to grow, that I
completely forgot my worries.

Luke 12:25-26

> "Can any of you by worrying add a
> single hour to your span of life? If then
> you are not able to do so small a thing
> as that, why do you worry about the
> rest?"

The Gift of a Child

A young couple I know tried for years to conceive a baby. They used almost every means at their disposal to encourage and guarantee conception. After many heartaches, the day finally came when they were blessed with a pregnancy. Everyone has showered them with best wishes and hope upon hope for a healthy and happy baby. After so many years of waiting, the proud parents-to-be under-standably want their child to be perfect and to enter as perfect a world as possible.

I, too, wish them the best. But I also hope that the child will have compassion for the sufferings of others. I hope that whatever happiness the child may know in this life will be the fruit of a search for God.

Such a search involves not only joy but no small amount of heartache. For it is through both glories and sorrows that our need for God, for a love larger than our own hearts, comes to fruition and we find our true birth in the God who made us.

Psalm 22:9

Yet it was you who took me from the
    womb;
    you kept me safe on my mother's
    breast.
On you I was cast from my birth,
    and since my mother bore me
        you have been my God.

THE KEEPSAKE

My twin brother Jimmy was killed in a car accident thirty-four years ago. My father kept Jimmy's wallet—which was found on him the night he died—in the top drawer of my parents' bureau until the day Dad died.

I now have the wallet. One night I looked through it. There were dance tickets and movie-theater stubs, phone numbers of girlfriends, ID cards and high school detention slips. But most of all there were the memories of Jimmy: his world of 1966, the way he walked and smiled, the way we grew up together. And now I think of Dad, too, who kept very few things over the years but treasured a lost son and his wallet. I am sure that there were nights he, too, sat in a chair near his bureau and looked through the wallet.

The wallet is in a little box in my room. The box is slightly larger than my heart, for the wallet is not too big. But it is a key now to my memories of Dad and Jimmy, who now live a new life in a place where keepsakes have their true and only meaning. We keep what we have of others until we see them again in a place where all that remains forever are God and each other.

LUKE 2:19

Mary treasured all these words and pondered them in her heart.

TREASURE

Each of us has what Abraham Maslow called "peak experiences," moments when life brims with goodness and wondrous possibilities. Some call them mystical experiences or experiences of the Divine. They occur when love is known as the deepest reality there is.

It would be marvelous if such experiences lasted through all our days. But life returns to its ordinary routine. We need reminders that the universe is God's field and the treasure beneath its soil is love. On those many days when we stand on shifting or fallow ground, it is good to ask for the faith to believe that love is not all that far beneath our feet.

MATTHEW **13:44**

"The kingdom of heaven is like treasure hidden in a field, which someone found and hid; then in his joy he goes and sells all that he has and buys that field."

Forget the Past

It is easy to let the past drag us down. I know a woman who makes all sorts of connections between things that happened years ago and problems that beset her now. I kid her a bit, and she lets up for a time. But it is not too long before I sense that she is again dredging up the past to explain some present ill.

Perhaps we hold on to the past because it is what we know. But God asks us to be attentive to the moment and look to the light of the future. The glimmer of the light and love that is God shines through each of us. And that light far outshines the dim and fading lights of the past.

Philippians 3:13

Beloved, I do not consider that I have made it my own; but this one thing I do: forgetting what lies behind and straining forward to what lies ahead.

THE AUTHOR OF THE UNIVERSE

Some writers like to pen letters before they begin their daily regimen of writing. It is a way to move slowly into the realm of more intensive writing.

I like to think of God as the writer who is writing creation. Perhaps God has begun the universe as a letter, prior to getting down to the more serious business of penning the Kingdom. Jesus is the Word, a living sign of more to come. To live a day is to live part of God's narrative. To love and be loved is to know something of the eternal outcome of the story.

JEREMIAH **31:33**

This is the covenant that I will make with the house of Israel after those days, says the LORD: I will put my law within them, and I will write it on their hearts; and I will be their God, and they shall be my people.

LATE THAW

It was the winter of 1965. My twin brother Jimmy and I shared a third-floor bedroom. We were seventeen years old. We leaned out the window and smoked a cigarette before crawling into our beds. We passed the glowing butt back and forth and chatted very quietly, since Mom and Dad's bedroom was just below ours. Then we spat on the butt and flicked it into the snow far below.

Spring came, the snow melted, and the evidence of our transgressions—hundreds of soggy cigarette butts—littered the grass below the window. Mom was not amused. We should have been smart enough to clean up our mess before Mom noticed it. But we had been counting on a late thaw.

MATTHEW 24:42

"Keep awake therefore, for you do not know on what day your Lord is coming."

WINKY DINK

When we were kids we used to watch a TV show called "Winky Dink," whose stated aim was to enhance the creativity of kids all over the country. The catch was that you had to send away for a special plastic screen. The screen was then taped across the TV set when the show was on. With special coloring pens that were also provided, a child could draw along with Winky Dink. Even though Winky Dink was broadcast from California, a kid could be in front of his or her TV set anywhere in the country and still participate, which seemed miraculous in those days.

In our house, unfortunately, the plastic screen soon cracked and was discarded, but the coloring pens remained. These were then applied directly to the TV set, and eventually to walls, doors, and floors by the Behrens kids.

Soon there was no more Winky Dink. Mom and Dad saw to that.

ISAIAH 1:18

Come now, let us argue it out,
    says the LORD:
though your sins are like scarlet,
    they shall be like snow;
though they are red like crimson,
    they shall become like wool.

Everything You Need

Our consumer culture creates one appetite after another urging us to buy this or that or go here or there to find ever-elusive human happiness.

There are not many places to go here at the monastery. Nor are there things to buy. There are no televisions or other distractions. The very nature of the place invites a monk to simply live with what is.

You can look at a fiery red sunrise and a golden sunset, and in between them live a day. And in that day you can think about God and realize that God isn't elusive. God is where you are. But maybe you have to turn the sound down a bit or relax quietly in your own backyard. Everything you really need is all there.

Philippians **4:19**

God will fully satisfy every need of yours according to his riches in glory in Christ Jesus.

You've Got Mail!

It is a thrill to key in a few simple strokes on a computer keyboard and in a matter of seconds be connected to the seemingly infinite expanse of cyberspace. There is a feeling of being in touch with something alive and active.

At daily Mass, surrounded as I am by very ordinary monks in very ordinary circumstances and bound to them and to God by vows, I see cyberspace reduced to the slow passage of time, the cadence of words, the occasional cough, sneeze, sniffle, the clearing of a throat, off-key singing, and the sound of sandaled feet on the hard floor of the church.

Sometimes the phrase, "You've got mail!" comes to my mind.

Matthew 18:20

"For where two or three are gathered in my name, I am there among them."

FIRE

One night one of our old barns at the monastery burned down. Most of the bonsai pots and tools we ship from the barn were destroyed. It took a year to recover.

The fire lasted no more than two hours, yet how many lives were affected by it—the brave firefighters and inspectors, the generous people who donated money, time, and prayer, the understanding customers who patiently waited for replacement shipments. The more I think about it, there is no end to tracing the effects of that one night.

The fire was devastating, but in its path came a shower of incredible goodness.

PSALM 50:3

> Our God comes and does not keep silence,
> before him is a devouring fire,
> and a mighty tempest all around him.

Abundance

I wanted a tube of shaving cream—the old-fashioned kind you work up in a cup. It was just a thing I was going through. I found none in the stores near the monastery, so I asked a pharmacist friend of mine if he could get any. He sent me twelve tubes. Enough to last me years!

A while later, I happened to mention to another pharmacist friend that I was surprised that tubes of shaving cream no longer seemed available on store shelves. Not long after, a box arrived in the mail with twelve *more* tubes of English shaving cream and a pig's hair shaving brush. Very fancy stuff—made for the King and Queen. (Or I guess just the King.)

Anyway, now I have enough shaving cream to last me till my death...and then some. This episode inspired the following poetic reflection:

> I have two fine friends who gathered me
>   lather,
> So I can be most generously slathered.
> Now I know why the King's face is fair,
> And some little piggies have not any hair.

MATTHEW 13:12

"For to those who have, more will be given, and they will have an abundance; but from those who have nothing, even what they have will be taken away."

LOVE BEYOND MEASURE

The sheer magnitude of the universe, the speed of light, the numbers of stars and galaxies is incomprehensible. On the "local" level things are no less overwhelmingly complex—the multitudes of people, their myriad hopes and desires, histories and languages.

If it were possible to weigh all these things, to somehow contain them in a sum or an equation, the figures would indeed be staggering.

But God's love, as the power and mystery behind it all, is what I like to contemplate as I ponder the vastness of things. Added all up, the swirl that fills the universe comes from God and is spinning toward God. And that swirl and spin are of a love that is far bigger than whatever can be measured.

JOB 26:13-14

> By his wind the heavens were made fair;
>   his hand pierced the fleeing serpent.
> These are indeed but the outskirts of his
>   ways;
>   and how small a whisper do we hear
>   of him!
>   But the thunder of his power who can
>   understand?

Not-So-Fast Friends

When I first moved here to the monastery, I looked around hoping to see among all the new faces those who would offer me friendship. What I failed to recognize were the crucial elements of time and patience in friend-making. The friendships I had back in New Jersey were deep because of the many years they had to develop.

I am learning patience here, with myself and with others. I now value the seconds, hours, days, and years, knowing that God is seeding them with the grace of good and lasting friendships. And as these friendships deepen, I am discovering that I never really left my old friends behind. They have made a home within me; their presence is just as real as my heart and memory.

JOHN 14:23

"Those who love me will keep my word, and my Father will love them, and we will come to them and make our home with them."

UNREHEARSED LIVES

As a parish priest, I discovered that most wedding rehearsals lasted far longer than the wedding itself. After going through the routine twice, nervous couples invariably wanted to go through it a third and even fourth time. I would tell them to just trust the ritual and relax. I don't think many of them heard a word I said.

Marriage, indeed life itself, has no rehearsals. But we do go through all sorts of preparations, day in and day out, to control our lives and make them as predictable and as tidy as possible.

But God is always in the strange and unexpected. Religious ritual ideally should open our hearts to the God who comes in ways we cannot plan. If our rituals suggest to us that enough practice will make everything turn out just as we planned, we are in the wrong church and worshiping a God who does not exist.

1 PETER 4:12

> Beloved, do not be surprised at the fiery ordeal that is taking place among you to test you, as though something strange were happening to you.

SERVICE WITH A SMILE

Jesus willingly gave himself to his disciples and to all of us as a farewell gift, but not before he taught us how to live joyfully with and for one another. The discovery of the self comes through service to others. We gain our lives by giving them away.

LUKE 22:26

"But not so with you; rather the greatest among you must become like the youngest, and the leader like one who serves."

Darkness, My Old Friend

On Good Friday, death is very close here at the monastery. A stillness permeates the day. The mystery of life takes on enormous proportions.

I sit in the woods on the monastery grounds and ask myself if death is something I can embrace, accepting it and living from that acceptance? Would I love more deeply and feel more at peace if I could?

In the darkness of this day I realize God befriended even death.

Luke 23:44

It was now about noon, and darkness fell over the whole land until three in the afternoon.

Two Lost Hats

The same train roared through the same tunnel at the same time every morning. He wore his favorite hat and leaned over the platform to see the oncoming train. When the train's last car roared past, a howling wind raced after it and blew the man's hat right off his bald head. He said a bad word and flung his paper to the ground. I watched the hat ride the winds as it made its merry way to a new life down the dark tunnel.

The man bought a new hat identical in every detail to the one he had lost. The very next day, the same train roared through the same tunnel. The man leaned over the platform to see the oncoming train, and it rushed past him as it did every morning. And when the train's last car cleared the platform, a howling wind raced after it and blew the man's new hat right off his bald head. He said the same bad word and flung his paper to the ground. I watched the hat ride the winds as it made its merry way to a new life down the dark tunnel.

I told the hatless man that maybe there was someone at the next spot who was tickled to death catching hats every morning. He was not amused.

SIRACH 7:8

Do not commit a sin twice;
   not even for one will you go
      unpunished.

Resurrection

Not ten feet from the rear porch of the monastery church lie the remains of our departed monks. They rest in the earth, and above them stretches the universe.

I believe that someday God will speak and my dead colleagues will rise—bones and all.

Ezekiel **37:3-4**

He said to me, "Mortal, can these bones live?" I answered, O Lord God, you know." Then he said to me, "Prophesy to these bones, and say to them: O dry bones, hear the word of the Lord. Thus says the Lord God to these bones: I will cause breath to enter you, and you shall live."

Community

God calls us all to live in community. Our salvation is realized in and through living with others. The Trinity is communal, and each of us reflects that related-ness. Grace builds on nature, and human nature is social.

Life at the monastery is stripped of many things that, while good in themselves, can distract us from the sense of community. Monks pray, work, and eat with each other. We become a part of each other in ways that would not be as clear or even as possible if we lived in different circumstances.

We have vowed to each other to stay here and to trust the presence of God in our lives. In many ways, we are like a family. We lay claim to each other in a deep and lasting way. In the simplicity of the life we live, we do not have much else to worry about other than our common aspiration: to listen with care to the God who is the foundation of our communal life.

ROMANS 15:7

Welcome one another, therefore, just as Christ has welcomed you, for the glory of God.

Traveling North

My colleague at the bonsai shop, Karen, received a call that her friend had died of an aneurysm. He was young, married with two sons. Karen and her husband, John, made plans to drive north to Minnesota to be with the man's family. People were coming from all parts of the country to mourn. Karen and John will stay for a while to be of whatever support they can.

One life is taken, and other lives hasten to give love and support.

It is cold in Minnesota. A young wife and her children need the warmth and comfort that is heading their way in the hearts of people who travel up from the South. God is good to inspire people to love so deeply.

Isaiah **40:1**

Comfort, O comfort my people,
says your God.

Significant Others

We have a lot of cats who hang out behind the retreat house. One afternoon I walked by as the cats were eating at a large tray beneath a tree. Individual rights were being respected according to some kind of hierarchy I have not quite figured out. Then I saw on the fringe of the crowd a small kitten. He tried once to get near the plate and was quickly hissed at and even bashed by a paw. I felt sorry for him but figured that he would have to learn cat ways.

Eventually he did. He is now part of the club and probably bashing other newcomers until they, too, achieve cat-world status.

I think the most unnerving aspect to the teaching and lifestyle of Jesus is his insistence that we love one another as brothers and sisters. His words demand that we level all distinctions. Hierarchies are not in the ordained order of things. Love is. To the extent that we make a reality out of our distinctions and an unreality out of love, we do not know much more than cats.

John 13:35

"By this everyone will know that you are my disciples, if you have love for one another."

BE STILL

The boy was five years old, waiting with his mother in a hospital clinic. I was in the same room for some tests results. He had to be given a shot in his arm. He squirmed and then screamed as he saw the nurse readying the needle. The nurse and his mother could not keep him still. "Helen, come in here for a minute," the nurse called out, and within seconds a large presence entered the room. Helen descended upon the boy, told him it would all be over in a second, and held him until the shot was administered.

Movement is essential to life, but every now and then situations arise that demand that we be still in order to grow and improve.

PSALM 46:10

> "Be still, and know that I am God!
> I am exalted among the nations,
> I am exalted in the earth."

Cast in the Shadows

While taking a walk around the monastery I noticed a very large tree, which was covered on one side with rich green leaves and on the other side was dark and barren. The side with all the life was facing the sun.

The tree cannot turn by itself to allow the sun to shine on its barren side. Despite that, it is a lovely tree. It's the way God made it.

That big tree serves as a reminder to me to be more patient with my dark side and the dark sides of others. We are lovely despite the parts of us cast in the shadows. It's the way God made us.

PSALM 121:5

The LORD is your keeper;
    the LORD is your shade at your right
       hand.

Luna Moth

It looked at first like a large green leaf, but when I
looked closer I saw that it was a luna moth. It had
just emerged from its cocoon and had instinctively
found a place in the sun, where it rose just a bit off
the ground and spread its wings to dry. I was
stunned by the small creature's instinct to turn
toward warmth. The light would soon dry those
glistening green wings, and then the moth would
take flight.

It seems to take human beings much longer
before we learn to find the light, turn to it, and
bask in its grace and wisdom. But in so doing, we
can find our true nature and the source of our
sustenance.

Psalm 4:6

> There are many who say, "O that we
>   might see some good!
>   Let the light of your face shine on us,
>   O Lord!"

THE ART OF SHARING

When I was a kid, we had one TV in our house. My four brothers and two sisters, Mom and Dad, and Grandma shared the same screen. There were many squabbles, usually settled by Dad or Mom in one of several ways. The first was to give each child the right to choose a show. Another was to overrule everyone and pick a show themselves. And the most effective way to settle a dispute was to clear the room—"Everyone out!"

Through it all, we kids learned the art of sharing and the wisdom of negotiation. Treaties and deals of all varieties were finessed. Since vengeance for reneging on contracts was swift, sure, and unpleasant, more often than not the deals stuck.

I was at a very different home several years ago. There were five children, and each had his or her own TV. I suppose that is another way of settling disputes, or avoiding them. But the price is far higher than the cost of all those TV sets.

HEBREWS **13:16**

Do not neglect to do good and to share what you have, for such sacrifices are pleasing to God.

WHERE WE COME FROM

I like the title of Raymond Carver's collection of
short stories, *Where I Am Calling From*. I bought
the book on the title alone, but the stories of where
people come from in terms of their hurts, hopes,
and need for love delivered as well.

What a gift it is to be able to see where people
come from—to see into their hearts and know
their stories. Jesus had this gift, which he shared
with us. He saw where people stood, where they
came from, and where they were called to go.

MARK 10:21

> Jesus, looking at him, loved him and
> said, "You lack one thing; go, sell what
> you own, and give the money to the
> poor, and you will have treasure in
> heaven; then come, follow me."

SOLITUDE

Great ideas demand great amounts of solitude to gestate. Time alone is never wasted if it eventually bears fruit in the lives of others.

Philosopher Alfred North Whitehead said, "Creativity is what one does with one's solitude." I picture that great thinker alone in his study working on his ideas and giving shape to his philosophy.

Our culture finds it increasingly more difficult to understand the solitary life. Yet, all genius requires solitude in its making.

LUKE 4:1

Jesus, full of the Holy Spirit, returned from the Jordan and was led by the Spirit in the wilderness.

What's Your Story?

Our worries build up to real problems when we do not share them with others. Therapists, counselors, and spiritual advisors encourage people to tell their stories in order to close certain chapters and write new endings. Telling our tales of woe to friends or family helps puts them in a more healthy perspective. Jesus, of course, was the master storyteller. He told us about our lives before we even lived them, and he wrote a new beginning for each of us.

MATTHEW **28:15**

This story is still told among the Jews to this day.

Delayed Response

I wrote to a poet named Nellie to tell her how much I liked one of her poems. Almost a year later I received a thank you note from her in the mail. I was glad she had responded and never once wondered why she had taken so long.

I just hope she wrote more poetry in the meantime.

ECCLESIASTES **3:1**

For everything there is a season, and a time
for every matter under heaven.

A GOOD NIGHT'S SLEEP

At times I fall asleep aware that, when I do sleep, God is awake and does not need me to keep the world going. To sleep is to trust. And to trust in God is to live a more peaceful life.

JEREMIAH **17:7-8**

Blessed are those who trust in the
    LORD,
        whose trust is the LORD.
They shall be like a tree planted by
    water,
        sending out its roots by the stream.
It shall not fear when heat comes,
        and it's leaves shall stay green;
    in the year of drought it is not anxious,
        and it does not cease to bear fruit.

Pocket Change

For as long as I can remember, I have walked looking at the ground. An occasional quick glance ahead of me is enough to keep me going where I need to go. I have seen so many things at my feet over the years. A twenty dollar bill on a street in New Orleans, a ten dollar bill in Manhattan. And ants galore, especially here at the monastery.

I wish that I lived as I walk. I tend to look too far down the road and worry about things I cannot even see—things that may never come to pass. Yet when I'm honest with myself, I know that I've gotten to where I was going without much planning. The important things have just been given as I walked my years, like found treasures on the ground.

Luke 10:41-42

"Martha, Martha, you are worried and distracted by many things; there is need of only one thing."

Waiting

We wait in patience for many things that we know will come: busses and planes, boats and trains, appointments, and special days on our calendar. Things of our own making are easy enough to await.

God apparently has a calendar, too. But it seems that it is laid out very differently from ours. To be human is to wait. God will bring goodness about according to eternal time and measure.

Psalm 40:1

I waited patiently for the Lord;
he inclined to me and heard my cry.

To Be of Good Heart

We are happiest, most ourselves, when we can give our hearts to someone. A good heart is one that receives love and expresses love.

Every activity that is performed with love begets love—cooking, singing, painting, listening, speaking, praying, caring, smiling, writing, reading. The human heart is vast. It is of God. Put heart in all that you do.

Psalm **86:11**

Teach me your way, O Lord,
    that I may walk in your truth;
    give me an undivided heart to revere
      your name.

ENCOURAGEMENT

Encouragement is a beautiful word meaning to *en couer,* to "give heart" or help the heart of another. What a lovely offering. Many people suffer from discouragement because of talents that go unrecognized or services that go unappreciated.

Every day presents opportunities to encourage the gifts of others.

To give heart to another enlarges one's own.

EPHESIANS **6:22**

I am sending him to you for this very purpose, to let you know how we are, and to encourage your hearts.

Finding God in New Ways

My friend is sad because he looked back on his life and could not be the way he was ten years ago. He hinted that he felt closer to God back then, for he prayed more readily and found it easier to read Scripture.

But perhaps my friend is being tested for a purpose. It could be that he does not recognize the fruits of his present life because they seem strange and not at all what he expected. My friend is being asked to find God in new ways these days.

He talks about these things, and people who love him help him along. His openness has helped others more than he knows.

Prayer and seeking provide many small miracles.

Matthew 7:7-8

"Ask, and it will be given you; search, and you will find; knock, and the door will be opened for you. For everyone who asks receives, and everyone who searches finds, and for everyone who knocks, the door will be opened."

CALLED BY NAME

With one word Jesus called Mary Magdalene to a new sense of identity. He called her by name, and her old world was obliterated, her life forever changed. Jesus spoke, and she turned.

Those two acts sum up the meaning of conversion. Jesus calls us each by name, and we respond. And then, like Mary, we run with joy to tell others.

JOHN **20:16**

Jesus said to her, "Mary!"

THE GOD OF STORY

From the time we are young, we listen to stories.

When we grow older, we realize that we are living one.

LUKE 24:32

They said to each other, "Were not our hearts burning within us while he was talking to us on the road, while he was opening the scriptures to us?"

BEHOLD YOUR MOTHER

While standing in an airport, my sister Mary placed my several-week-old nephew in my arms while she went off to attend to her ticket.

He watched her as she left, his little bald head turning and following her every move. He started to cry when she was out of sight. He squirmed in my arms and found peace again only when she neared. I was amazed at how a little baby already possessed such powers of recognition. Mary laughed and said, "I am his mother."

In the same way, God is our mother. God's image is imprinted in our hearts, and we seek the one who fashioned that image our whole lives. Perhaps human compassion is our attempt to help one another deal with the perceived temporary absence of God.

LUKE 2:45

When they did not find him, they returned to Jerusalem to search for him.

The Word Was Made Flesh

It is a year today that her young son took his own life. She was at Vigils this morning, as she has been many a morning this past year. I have heard her cry. But I have also seen her smile a beautiful smile.

The man next to her lost his place in the psalm book. In the dim light of the church, she saw and moved toward him and with her finger pointed out the right line of the text. The words of that psalm took flesh right before my eyes.

May the movement of her heart toward another return to her and sustain her in the darkness she feels. Touch her, Lord, and become flesh for her as she was for another.

Luke 6:19

All in the crowd were trying to touch him,
for power came out from him and healed
all of them.

And God Said

My mom told me to sit and not move until she said so. Thus it was from a chair in a corner, my eyes looking at the wall, that I first pondered the power of language.

Today as I think of all that is, from the wondrous array of stars in the sky this early morning hour to the sweet chirping of a bird I hear now outside my window, I am in awe that everything came from the Word of God. God spoke, and all is.

What is this divine language of being? I want to know something of its grammar and vocabulary. I would gladly spend my life learning to speak a language where words create reality.

Genesis 1:3

Then God said, "Let there be light"; and there was light.

Light Your Fire

Dryness of heart has no better remedy than prayer.

It is like asking God for a match.

Psalm 102:4

My heart is stricken and withered like grass.

In God's Time

Every morning at Lauds, the first chant is "Lord, make haste to help me." Not only do we ask the Lord to come, but we ask that it be done quickly.

That petition has been chanted for more than a thousand years, several times a day, in monasteries all over the world.

God made time and all that comes with it: eons and centuries and gray hair and wrinkles and feet that shuffle. So maybe on God's time, salvation is speeding along just fine.

Psalm 70:1

> Be pleased, O God, to deliver me.
> O Lord, make haste to help me!

MR. ALLIGATOR

My three-year-old niece Molly was sucking her thumb as she walked alongside me by a lake shore in southern Louisiana. It was a beautiful, peaceful day. While taking in her thumb and the world about her, Molly noticed a ripple in the water, far off shore.

It was an alligator.

"Hello, Mr. Alligator," she said, without even taking her thumb out of her mouth. She pointed with her pinky in the direction of Mr. Alligator. For a moment I was terrified, but the thing glided along, placing us out of harm's way.

Her innocence amazed me: seeing something so exotic and calling to it like an old friend.

May Molly's heart always be as open to the stranger as it was that day. May she delight in all creatures of God...yet keep a wise distance from those who may not wave back in like fashion.

ISAIAH **11:8**

The nursing child shall play over the hole
of the asp,
and the weaned child shall put its
hand on the adder's den.

BROKEN HEARTS

The body of Jesus is able to be shared because it was broken.

This day I ask a blessing on all hearts that will break. I will be thankful for broken hearts, for only a broken heart can be shared.

MARK 14:22

> While they were eating, he took a loaf of bread, and after blessing it he broke it, gave it to them, and said, "Take; this is my body."

For Crying Out Loud

Why are so many people, particularly men, afraid of crying? How many of us have sat in the movies, taking a peek at the person next to us to check for tears? We have an apparent aversion to or voyeuristic interest in signs of human weakness.

Jesus wept, according to the Gospel of John, after hearing of his friend Lazarus' death.

Were Jesus to break down and weep this day over the death of a friend, would we give him a side glance and quietly wonder about his strength or masculinity?

His tears are an invitation to all of us to look deeply into ourselves. We cannot reap life's greatest treasures without sharing in the mysterious sadness of a God who has shed tears.

JOHN **11:35**

Jesus began to weep.

Dying Our Deaths

He had lived a long and good life and was now dying in a hospital room. I was there with his son, a friend of mine who is a priest. The old man breathed heavily, and I asked my friend if there was anything that could be done. He smiled and said no, that his father was at peace. He told me that he and his dad had shared in the Eucharist just a short while before. Then my friend said, "The Lord is dying in him, and will also rise."

Never before had those words and their meaning hit me with such force. Our lives are not absolutely our own. Our births, our deaths, and the many sighs in between are of the very life of God, who lives in us and shall rise in us.

1 Peter 4:13

But rejoice that you participate in the sufferings of Christ, so that you may be overjoyed when his glory is revealed.

ORGANIZED THOUGHTS

I do not pass one of the ant mounds that abound in the state of Georgia without failing to admire the insects' organizational skills. Ants are among the most efficient creatures on earth.

Likewise, I look to the stars at night and feel awe at the order in the universe. Its precision defies comprehension.

And I stand there in between these two inspiring, ingeniously structured worlds and say a prayer that a little bit of its efficiency and precision will fall on me from above or travel up to me from below.

PROVERBS **6:6**

Go to the ant, you lazybones;
   consider its ways and be wise!

AT THE CENTER OF THINGS

Mornings at the monastery are silent—a time for pondering the center of things. I believe that the center of the universe intersects in the human heart.

I write and read in the early morning and at times pause and think of my mom and dad with love and longing. I feel very close to them despite eternal and temporal distance—closer than if they were sitting with me in this room.

A brother monk sits near me reading and writing. In our silence I sense the love in my heart and in my brother's. We are close to the center—much closer than the short physical distance between us.

LUKE **10:28**

"Do this, and you shall live."

Who Shall Be First?

Their rising voices could be heard throughout the crowded church. As I said the opening prayer, two women who were assigned as Eucharistic ministers for the Mass were arguing in the sacristy about who was supposed to give the chalice and who was to distribute from the ciborium. Appeals were thrown back and forth: the authority of the pastor, the misplaced assignment list, who did what the last time. Everyone in the church started to chuckle, and I was not about to play the role of Solomon and leave the altar to offer wisdom.

An accord was finally reached and the women paraded out to deliver communion, unaware that everyone had heard their arguing.

Each of us is called to serve. *How* we serve, or *what* we serve is secondary. I need not even have preached that day. The gospel had unfolded before our ears.

Luke 22:24

A dispute also arose among them as to which one of them was to be regarded as the greatest.

SPOKEN WORDS

One of our extroverted monks (yes, there are some) explained his need to say things out loud while he is sorting out his thoughts. It's as if he is placing the words before himself on an imaginary shelf so that he can see them and arrange them to his liking. Verbalizing what he feels has a transformative power.

God, then, must be the ultimate extrovert, for God speaks and his Word transforms us all.

JOHN 1:1-2

In the beginning was the Word, and the Word was with God, and the Word was God. He was in the beginning with God.

Washed Clean

I remember Dad washing my face and ears when I was little. He was not as gentle as Mom, and he scrubbed my face with what felt like the same force he used to wax the car. The finishing touch was when he parted my hair, brushed it, and slicked it down so hard it stayed that way for hours.

I could not have understood back then how deeply he loved us and how proud he was of us. I can see now, by looking at old photographs. how he and Mom beamed as they stood behind us seven gleaming children.

Dad scrubbed my face until it shined. It hurt a bit. To be loved by God until we shine can also hurt a bit, but I have to believe God is proud of us.

John 13:8-9

Peter said to him, "You will never wash my feet." Jesus answered, "Unless I wash you, you have no share with me." Simon Peter said to him, "Lord, not my feet only but also my hands and my head!"

THAT ALL MAY BE ONE

I heard a priest give a homily on the Catholic teaching of the Real Presence in the Eucharist. He said that this is the main theological difference that separates Catholics from Protestants. The irony of it struck me. What was and is given to unify all God's people has become a central divisive point.

I hope God has a sense of humor and patience while we take our sweet time learning to become one.

JOHN 17:23

> "I in them and you in me, that they may become completely one, so that the world may know that you have sent me and have loved them even as you have loved me."

Ancient Truth

What if Jesus had grown old and utterly dependent on the kindness and patience of others? What if he were an aged Messiah, no longer one of marvelous words and power but a frail ancient who needed others in order to make his way through a day?

I think about this as I work in the infirmary today. I will stay with Joe, one of our aging monks, for a while. He has been so tired lately.

John 4:6

Jacob's well was there, and Jesus, tired as he was from the journey, sat down by the well.

Usher in the Present

A woman I know once confided in me that she was terrified of her husband because he beat her.

That was many years ago. They have since divorced. She told me that while she was going through the trauma of coping with that abuse, her mind was never on the present. She would roam the past for comfort and the future for hope. A wise and forceful therapist eased her gently back into the present, from where she made her decision to end the marriage.

Love ushers us into the present moment, to respond to it with faith, hope, and strength.

1 John 4:18

There is no fear in love, but perfect love casts out fear; for fear has to do with punishment, and whoever fears has not reached perfection in love.

CONVERSION

Ernst Cassirer is a philosopher best known for his brilliant but heavy three-volume work, *Philosophy of Symbolic Forms*.

In the introduction, Cassirer writes that the idea for the theme of his work came to him while he was waiting to board a trolley car in Vienna. Why it happened on that day, and in that way, we will never know.

Conversion acts like that. It is a process that starts below the surface of our conscious thought, and then suddenly—whether we are riding to Damascus or boarding a Viennese trolley—it strikes us and sets us on a new course.

ACTS **9:3-4**

Now as he was going along and approaching Damascus, suddenly a light from heaven flashed around him. He fell to the ground and heard a voice saying to him, "Saul, Saul, why do you persecute me?"

An Audience with Jesus

I imagine myself standing before Jesus, putting on my best front while I talk nervously about the weather and sports.

He responds by reminding me of all the things I would prefer not to discuss—especially the hurts and wrongs I've done. But he speaks out of love, and through his love he shows me who I am in God's eyes. I am overwhelmed with joy by the beauty I see in myself.

JOHN **4:39**

Many Samaritans from that city believed in him because of the woman's testimony, "He told me everything I have ever done."

CHILDREN OF GOD

God shares our nature. Imagine that. God actually became human. The boy Jesus grew, like any one of us, with all the hopes and disappointments that human growth entails. And through Jesus, God transformed the meaning and promise of human life for all of us.

Teach a child today of his or her divine inheritance.

LUKE 2:40

The child grew and became strong, filled with wisdom; and the favor of God was upon him.

Take Heed!

"Don't touch, it's hot!" is one of countless warnings that every child has heard from his or her exasperated parents. Our endless curiosity draws us to touch hot things, eat dirt, and test the raging waters for ourselves.

Once we're grown, however, who warns us of the dangers before us?

The answer depends on who—and what—we believe.

Psalm **95:7-8**

O that today you would listen to his
voice!
Do not harden your hearts.

Taking Turns

When we ask that our lives be turned toward God, we expect to be turned in a peaceful way. But being at peace does not mean being at rest. Turning your direction toward God means constantly changing your course to serve others—a friend in need, a coworker out of sorts, a loved one in bad health. Turning toward God means always turning toward others—and that is not always an easy or comfortable task.

Isaiah **45:22**

Turn to me and be saved,
    all the ends of the earth!
    For I am God, and there is no other.

SLOW BURN

The day after Pentecost is a traditional day off here at the monastery. There are no work periods. We have the usual Mass and prayer services, a talking meal, and a movie at night.

I went down to the woods early this morning. It had rained last night, so the leaves and bushes above and about me glistened and sparkled. The sunlight seemed especially generous this morning.

Looking around me, I saw the world dazzling in its natural beauty. Like the Spirit within us, creation is a slow burn, but burn it does. All the manifestations of love this day are embers from the eternal fire of love.

ACTS 2:2-3

And suddenly from heaven there came a
sound like the rush of a violent wind,
and it filled the entire house where they
were sitting. Divided tongues, as of fire,
appeared among them, and a tongue
rested on each of them.

THE TEARS OF BIRTH

I have read that some poets cry as they write, as if the labor involved in giving birth to truly beautiful words from the depths of their hearts is a painful process not unlike birthing a child.

We often look to faith to give us security, ease our doubts, and soothe away our troubles. Yet if we live by the Word within us we may, like the poets, cry at its painful beauty and truth.

JOHN 1:14

The Word became flesh and lived among us, and we have seen his glory, the glory of a father's only son, full of grace and truth.

Neon

Being from a big city, I miss neon lights. We do not have any neon here at the monastery, and I suppose absence makes the heart grow fonder—even for the strangest things.

Yet our monastery is a welcoming place, so maybe some day we can put a deep blue neon sign on the lonely stretch of highway just outside our monastery walls that would read, "Welcome Traveler"—a bright Trappist light in a sometimes dim world.

Matthew 5:14

"You are the light of the world. A city built on a hill cannot be hid."

Full of Grace

We Trappists chant the Magnificat every evening.
The melody is exquisite, as are the words. The first
line, "My soul magnifies the Lord," is an invitation to
sing in gratitude for and to Mary, whose "yes" to God
gives each of us hope to utter "yes" with our own
lives.

There are no such things as empty days, even
though we may feel that there are. Each day is a
vessel filled with grace. The Lord has indeed done
great things for us, and the Son of God suffers, dies,
and rises through us. We raise our hearts to God
each evening, hoping that we, like Mary, may accept
God's presence in us and be faithful servants of the
Lord each day.

Luke 1:49

"For the Mighty One has done great
things for me,
and holy is his name."

In Due Time

I find it heartening that when the tax collector, Levi, was called by Jesus and supposedly left everything to follow him, he apparently kept his house and enough provisions to throw a great banquet in Jesus' honor.

It takes time to leave everything. Just ask any monk.

LUKE 5:29

Then Levi gave a great banquet for him in his house; and there was a large crowd of tax collectors and others sitting at the table with them.

THE LIGHT IN HIS EYES

The man was old and blind and ran a pet store not far from where I lived as a boy. He gave me my first job. I cleaned the cages and swept the floors.

He was a popular storyteller in the neighborhood. His sightless eyes moved and widened as he slowly told unforgettable stories of his past. He saw with a light more real and lasting than that given off by any star.

ISAIAH **60:19**

The sun shall no longer be
    your light by day,
nor for brightness shall the moon
    give light to you by night,
but the LORD will be your everlasting light,
    and your God will be your glory.

THE LOST HEART

While walking on one of our monastery roads, I found a shiny metal heart. I stooped to pick it up and admire it. It had not been there long. Not a speck of dirt was on it.

I placed a note on the bulletin board, and before the day was out a fellow monk approached me, said it had fallen out of his pocket, and thanked me. It was, he said, special to him. I was happy the little heart had found its rightful owner.

I believe that God is above all else a seeker of hearts. Even though mine may sometimes feel lost, I trust that God will search for it and return it to its proper place.

EZEKIEL **36:26**

A new heart I will give you, and a new spirit I will put within you; and I will remove from your body the heart of stone and give you a heart of flesh.

STILL LIFE

Down near one of the monastery lakes is a spot that is good for just sitting and looking out over the water. Not long ago, on a still day that reflected a stillness in my heart, I was able to ponder all the love that is in the world—present in as many ways as there are possibilities of people finding it and giving it to one another.

Suddenly a sharp sound of slapping water startled me out of my reverie. A goose had decided to make a very noisy crash landing into the lake. Water splashed in every direction. His friends followed fast and furiously. I kissed my beloved stillness good-bye.

Yet I know that stillness, like the love I was pondering, is a gift. It will return again to those waters, and love will rise again in my heart.

PSALM **131:2**

I have calmed and quieted my soul.

HOPE

Another monk was talking, but my mind was elsewhere. All the while he was present to me, I was not really listening to him. I caught myself and apologized. He smiled and said he understood.

How often I do that to God as well. God is present always, even though there are many times I am far from being aware of it. I hope God—like that gracious monk—smiles and understands.

ROMANS 5:5

> Hope does not disappoint us, because God's love has been poured into our hearts through the Holy Spirit that has been given to us.

People of the Word

We Christians are a people of the Word—spoken words and written ones—shared, handed down, loved, and taken to heart. We know ourselves and our God through the mystery of hearing, remembering, telling, and recording. The Word creates us, renews us, strengthens us, and brings us joy.

1 John 1:3-4

We declare to you what we have seen and heard so that you also may have fellowship with us; and truly our fellowship is with the Father and with his Son Jesus Christ. We are writing these things so that our joy may be complete.

COME UNTO ME

I was taking a walk on a gorgeous sunny day at the monastery. I looked about me and suddenly realized that God dreamed up all of creation. Our world is God's dream come true.

JOEL 2:28

Then afterward
   I will pour out my spirit on all flesh;
your sons and your daughters shall
      prophesy,
   your old men shall dream dreams,
   and your young men shall see visions.

MEDITATION ON A WASP

A wasp alighted on the edge of an old pipe next to where I was sitting. I looked at it and wondered how many millions of years of evolution it had taken to produce this particular specimen. A wasp cannot be explained apart from God's creation of time, the sun, the seasons, the food chain, and the climate.

I watched the small creature ascend toward a flickering light. Neither his flight to the light nor his very existence is less a mystery than mine.

DANIEL 2:17

Then the mystery was revealed to Daniel in a vision of the night, and Daniel blessed the God of heaven.

TOUGH LOVE

A mourning dove hatched in a nest on a window sill outside the cloister. I watched as its mother made trips to and fro to feed it. She would digest the food and then, with startling violence, regurgitate it down the throat of her chick. The chick did not seem to mind as it opened its mouth wide to receive the onslaught of its mother's generosity.

God is no less forceful in some of the ways love is poured into our hearts.

LUKE 12:24

"Consider the ravens: they neither sow nor reap, they have neither storehouse nor barn, and yet God feeds them. Of how much more value are you than the birds!"

BACKWARD VIEW

My friend took a trip to her native Ireland. When she entered the town she had last seen as a little girl, she was astonished at the changes. For days, she commented on everything she saw, saying things were better the way she remembered them. The visit embittered her. Sadly, she missed the present beauty because she looked only for the past.

ECCLESIASTES **7:10**

Do not say, "Why were the former days
  better than these?"
  For it is not from wisdom that you
  ask this.

Good Move

A three-year-old crawled into my lap as I sat listening to a family tell stories of a beloved eighty-year-old woman whom they had just waked. As I listened to one story after another, my eyes filled up and I brushed away tears. The little boy looked at me, at first bewildered but then understanding. "Don't be sad," he said, and then he gave me a kiss on the cheek. Everyone in the room saw what he had done and laughed. The little boy laughed, too, and kissed me again, sure that he had done something especially good.

He had.

PSALM **119:28**

My soul melts away for sorrow;
strengthen me according to your
word.

Survival Instincts

The kittens were only a few weeks old. Their mother had left them in the safety of the bushes in front of the monastery while she had gone off to feed. I did not want to alarm them but saw that I already had. They huddled together in one furry ball and shuddered, looking at me with fear and dread. They did not take their eyes off of me. I quietly left them, sensing that I was causing them much distress for their tender age.

Wouldn't it be wonderful, as Barry Lopez once observed, to be able to approach animals and have them respond with wonder and friendship. But long-standing experience causes them to recoil from humans to preserve themselves from death.

Genesis 9:2

"The fear and dread of you shall rest on every animal of the earth, and on every bird of the air, on everything that creeps on the ground, and on all the fish of the sea; into your hand they are delivered."

In Their Memory

Countless men and women have died in this century for what they believed would secure peace. How best to remember them? Live the hope for which they died.

Sirach 43:12

May their bones send forth new life
from where they lie,
and may the names of those who
have been honored
live again in their children!

Happy Birthday

I was born on May 31, 1948 in Brooklyn, New York.
Like any baby, I was brought into the world totally
dependent on the love of others for all my needs.
Loving a baby is a joyful and painful process—similar
to giving birth. All that we are, we owe to God and to
those who clothed and fed us, nurtured and pro-
tected us, and shaped and molded us by their loving
example. A birthday is any day we are given love
and give love.

Blessings to all babies born this day.

Blessings to all who are given love this day.

Blessings to all who love others and help them grow
this day.

John 3:4

Nicodemus said to him, "How can anyone
be born after having grown old? Can one
enter a second time into the mother's
womb and be born?"

MAY I JOIN YOU?

The young man came into the dining room of the retreat house and sat down by himself. I was sitting with a friend. He looked over and smiled. Then he got up and came over to our table and said softly, "Do you mind if I join you?"

"Of course not," I replied, and we made room for him at our table. We ate together, chatted a bit, and got to know each other.

I thought of him throughout the day. He was so obviously in need of conversation and friendship. He brought to my mind a sense of Jesus, who approached others for food and for friendship. Jesus liked being with people.

Saint Benedict admonished monks to welcome others who come to us as we would welcome Christ himself. We need to remember that Jesus was truly human, so very like you and me.

LUKE 24:41-43

> While in their joy they were disbelieving
> and still wondering, he said to them,
> "Have you anything here to eat?"
> They gave him a piece of broiled fish,
> and he took it and ate in their presence.

All That Matters

There are times at night, before I fall off to sleep, that I look back on the day and think about what I accomplished—as if life were a matter of stacking up all that I have done like so many trophies.

There are other nights when it is not my accomplishments I ponder but God's. It's then that I realize that what God does is all that matters.

Isaiah **55**:10-11

For as the rain and the snow come down
        from heaven
    and do not return there until they
        have watered the earth,
making it bring forth and sprout,
    giving seed to the sower and bread
        to the eater,
so shall my word be that goes out from
    my mouth;
    it shall not return to me empty,
but it shall accomplish that which I
    purpose,
        and succeed in the thing for which
            I sent it.

THE OLD MAN AND HIS FRIEND

An old man called the bonsai shop at the monastery and said that his friend had passed away and left him a favorite plant to care for. He needed help with the plant. How much water did it need? What kind of soil? How much sun?

I told the man what I knew about such things and then asked him when his friend had passed away. He told me that it had been very recently and then he started to cry softly.

That was five years ago, and I have thought of that old man many times since. I hope his bonsai plant is doing well. If he cared for it as much as he cared for his friend, I am sure it is thriving.

We seem to know what is best for that which we love.

MATTHEW 7:9-11

"Is there anyone among you who, if your child asks for bread, will give a stone? Or if the child asks for a fish, will give a snake?"

Exalted States

A flower is simply itself; it need not be anything more or less. It reveals all the glory of God in the singularity of its beauty. A flower waving to and fro in the wind is its own hymn to God.

A human is beautiful in being human. We, too, sway in the wind and are no less a song to God.

PSALM 9:2

I will be glad and exult in you;
    I will sing praise to your name,
        O Most High.

MYSTERIOUS PRESENCE

My dear friend has told me many times that he wished he had made the trip to be with me when I was in a lot of pain. But the pain had come on fast, and there was no time for him to reach me.

I thought of him a lot during those days. I missed him but felt his presence deeply. During the Eucharist one morning, I felt completely connected to my friend, and I was overwhelmed with gratitude to the Lord who made us like that. Indeed, it struck me that the most enduring presence of those we love is not achieved through traveling miles or spending hours on the phone. Through the gift of many years of friendship, my friend is a part of me in a beautiful and mysterious way. That intricate, inextricable bond is what God creates through human love.

PSALM **16:11**

> You show me the path of life.
>   In your presence there is fullness
>   of joy;
>   in your right hand are pleasures
>   forevermore.

Process Theology

What does it take to make a unique and beautiful bonsai pot? The type of wood, the amount of moisture in the wood, the intensity and duration of the heat in a fiery kiln, the position of the pot during firing, the structure of the kiln—all these things and more—work together along with the artistry of the potter. No one element of this process can be understood apart from the others.

So, too, with God's creation.

Job 37:14-15

"Hear this, O Job;
　　　　stop and consider the wondrous
　　　　　　works of God.
Do you know how God lays his
　　　　command upon them,
　　　　and causes the lightning of his
　　　　　　cloud to shine?"

GOD THE TRAPPER

There are times in our lives when we wonder what God thinks about who we are and what we do or don't do.

Try as we might to follow the Lord, we get caught in some awful snares. But maybe that is right where God has asked us to go.

HOSEA 1:2-3

When the LORD first spoke through Hosea, the LORD said to Hosea, "Go, take for yourself a wife of whoredom and have children of whoredom, for the land commits great whoredom by forsaking the LORD." So he went and took Gomer daughter of Diblaim, and she conceived and bore him a son.

MAKING FRIENDS

I was in fifth grade when we moved to a new town. I sat on the back steps of our new house and soon the kid from next door came over. His name was Peter. He wore two casts, one on each arm, from a fall he had taken out of the tree. He said he had just moved, too. We became fast friends and remain so to this day.

That's how it is with God, too. He sits on the steps of our lives every day, seeking our friendship.

SIRACH 25:9

Happy is the one who finds a friend,
and the one who speaks to
attentive listeners.

STAY

I cannot think of a more eloquent prayer than "Stay." The presence of the Lord is all that matters.

LUKE 24:29

They urged him strongly, "Stay with us, for it is nearly evening; the day is almost over." So he went in to stay with them.

Bird Song

There are days when, even at dawn, everything ahead feels like a burden.

I sit still on such mornings and listen to the birds as they start their day. It is dark, and stars are yet visible, but their songs are strong and full of what sounds to me like happiness.

Perhaps God created such beauty to remind me that most of the work of the day ahead can only be accomplished with the help of others—just as the birds have helped raise my burdened spirits with their morning symphony.

Lamentations 3:22-23

The steadfast love of the Lord never
ceases,
his mercies never come to an end;
they are new every morning;
great is your faithfulness.

ENTER MY HEART

I know of no greater human experience than that of asking God to enter my heart and teach me the wisdom of silent and faithful loving.

PSALM 51:6
_____

You desire truth in the inward being;
therefore teach me wisdom
in my secret heart.

The Coyote in Manhattan

Everything around him was alien. So he ran and ran and ended up in Central Park, right in the middle of Manhattan. He was a lonesome and frightened coyote.

People took pity on him. They tranquillized him, wrapped him in a blanket, and took him to safety. Later they released him in a place where he would be able to find coyote kin.

Salvation in Central Park.

Something of me in that coyote.

Something of God in those who saved him.

Psalm 7:1

O Lord my God, in you I take refuge;
    save me from all my pursuers, and
        deliver me.

Slow Light

Light can now be slowed to thirty-two miles an hour, or so I recently read in the paper.

Maybe a seat can be made—a very light one—so that you can ride a moonbeam or, if you can take the heat, a sunbeam.

Or perhaps you can catch a falling star and put it in your pocket.

Better yet, become a bit of light yourself and love someone today.

Job 38:24

"What is the way to the place where the
light is distributed,
or where the east wind is scattered
upon the earth?"

I Love New York

I used to live close enough to Manhattan that I could see the skyline from my bedroom window. It was beautiful at night. Yet I was aware that the lights, the skyscrapers, the sense of enormity and grandeur that is Manhattan could easily obscure all that was taking place in its buildings and on its streets. There is much sadness in that city. Just to gaze out my window was a meditation on what it means to be human.

Loving a place like New York City helps me to love myself better. I look inside myself and know there is sadness, but there is also joy and light—and perhaps on occasion from a distance at night—I even look beautiful!

PROVERBS **19:8**

To get wisdom is to love oneself.

For All the People

The Word of the Lord was often addressed to individuals, but in every case the Word thus given was for all the people.

The gathering that we call church is the sacrament of the social. Even those who choose to live apart, such as monks, are in communion with the greater community. Like an artist standing back to get a better perspective on an object, the solitary man or woman withdraws in order to bring himself or herself closer to all the people.

Isaiah 40:3

"In the wilderness prepare the way
of the Lord,
make straight in the desert a
highway for our God."

In Harm's Way

I saw a mother bird fly into the branches of a box-
wood tree. I approached the nest, peeked in, and
saw her sitting on two chicks, their tiny heads visible
beneath her. She became frantic, flew to the ground,
and feigned being wounded to distract me from the
two young babies. She moved further and further
away from the nest. I made a hasty retreat, not
wanting to cause any harm to her or her young. She
flew back to the nest when she sensed that it was
safe.

How strong is creation's need to protect vulnerable
life from harm. That mother bird made me think
about how I must make myself vulnerable in order to
help others.

2 Corinthians 11:29

Who is weak, and I am not weak? Who is
made to stumble, and I am not indignant?

Wipe Away Our Tears

I am haunted by a picture I saw on the front page of the *New York Times*. It was of an old man wiping his tears with his hand. He had lost his house and all that he owned following the bombing of the city where he lived. I cut the picture out and placed it on my desk. I am saddened that I cannot be of comfort to the mourning man. I pray that he be given shelter and all that he needs to once again live a good life. I trust that the Lord will hear my prayers.

Psalm 34:18

The Lord is near to the broken
hearted,
and saves the crushed in spirit.

Words of Comfort

Augustine, one of the oldest monks in the cloister, was going through a book that he had kept for years, and from its pages fell a photograph of his parents. He showed the Abbot the photo, and as he was telling him the story of how the long lost picture fell from the book, he started to cry.

When my dad died and I returned to the monastery after staying with my mom, this same gentle, soft-hearted monk had hugged me and said, "Welcome home." I needed to hear that from him on that day.

When I heard of Augustine's sadness, I went to him and finally thanked him for his kindness to me. I hope it was something he needed to hear that day.

Psalm 27:7

Hear O Lord, when I cry aloud,
　　　be gracious to me and answer me!

Peace Be with You

The first word that the risen Jesus speaks to his disciples is "Peace."

In giving peace to his disciples, and to us, Jesus gives his very self. The gift of his peace is a share in his life, his very person. Peace is not something we bring into being as the result of treaties or prolonged periods of calm. Peace is Jesus. Peace is a person. Peace is the gift of his life.

John 20:19

> When it was evening on that day, the first day of the week, and the doors of the house where the disciples had met were locked for fear of the Jews, Jesus came and stood among them and said, "Peace be with you."

Promise

When I was young, my friends and I made vows and "crossed our hearts and hoped to die" if we broke them. We took promises very seriously.

As I've grown old, I realize just how important promises still are to me. I entrust my entire life to God's promise to be faithful. I know God is trustworthy, I will try to be, too—cross my heart.

Psalm 12:6

The promises of the LORD are promises
    that are pure,
      silver refined in a furnace on the
      ground,
      purified seven times.

DREAM LIFE

My grandmother lived to be ninety-four. She told me once that her years passed as quickly as a dream. I am learning from my own experience how fast the years go by. I try to remember that a full life is not one of many years but of living each day to the fullest. My grandmother befriended time and was grateful for all that time gave her. Throughout her life, joy came as a gift from a passing dream.

PSALM 39:4-5

"LORD, let me know my end,
  and what is the measure of my days;
  let me know how fleeting my life is.
You have made my days a few
    handbreadths,
  and my lifetime is as nothing in your
    sight.
Surely everyone stands as a
    mere breath."

SWIMMING LESSON

Dad taught me how to swim. I remember him holding me just above the water and then slowly letting me down into the surf. He told me to relax. I squirmed and moved my legs as fast as I could, more out of fear than any attempt to tread water. Yet he was right. As long as I relaxed, my fear went away and staying afloat was as natural as breathing.

Life is like the sea. The key to immersing yourself in it is twofold: relax and remember that one who cares is right there with you.

PSALM **139:9-10**

If I take the wings of the morning
    and settle at the farthest limits of the
      sea
even there your hand shall lead me,
    and your right hand shall hold me
      fast.

What's the Point?

While sitting on a bench one summer afternoon in Washington Square Park in New York City's Greenwich Village, I witnessed life in all its diversity—musicians, fire eaters, jugglers, acrobats, card players, Gypsies, ice cream vendors, kids playing ball, old men playing bocci, college students studying, young couples kissing, old couples holding hands, men selling incense, people walking their dogs.

I wrote an essay about all that I saw and tried to get it published. It was rejected. The editor said that there was no point to it. So I went back to the park looking for the point. But there was no point that I could see—just the park and all its kisses and wonders and beauty.

Maybe that was the point.

Acts **26:16**

"I have appeared to you for this purpose, to appoint you to serve and testify to the things in which you have seen me and to those in which I will appear to you."

HOUSE GUEST

Creation is God's house, and we are all welcomed guests. Upon our arrival, we tend to watch and follow the lead of others. We learn all sorts of formal prayers that are said in the hope of putting us at ease.

As the years pass, and our surroundings become familiar to us, we relax and open up. Our lives become a conversation with God. We chat easily. God has made us feel at home.

ROMANS **14:3**

God has welcomed them.

There's a Call for You

Poor Jonah. The Lord called and he ran away. But by fleeing, he caused himself a boatload of problems.

Often we hurl ourselves into seas of busyness, small talk, material pleasures, and elusive dreams to escape God's call to be fully human and to recognize the humanity of others. These busy things don't free us, they swallow us whole. God will continue to call, and eventually, like Jonah, we will learn the wisdom of answering.

Jonah 1:1-3

Now the word of the LORD came to Jonah son of Amittai, saying, "Go a once to Ninevah, that great city, and cry out against it; for their wickedness has come up before me." But Jonah set out to flee to Tarshish from the presence of the LORD.

PEE WEE

Pee Wee and I wrap bonsai pots together. He is a layman who grew up not far from the monastery. I love his laugh and like to listen to him talk. He has not had an easy go of it in life. But there is something about him that is very sound.

I asked Pee Wee recently what kind of person reminded him of God. He thought for just a few seconds and said with a smile, "A man of joy. A joyful man. That man knows God."

God has given Pee Wee a truthful heart and an appetite for joy. How close, then, God is to me in the mornings down at the bonsai barn.

PSALM 47:1

Clap your hands, all you peoples;
     shout to God with loud songs of joy.
For the LORD, the Most High, is
          awesome,
     a great king over all the earth.

WOULD YOU BE SO KIND?

Poet William Carlos Williams said that it is strange that so many people ignore poetry, when there are millions who suffer every day from the lack of poetry's wisdom.

The same can be said of kindness.

PROVERBS 21:21
_____

Whoever pursues righteousness and
kindness
will find life and honor.

What Is, Was, and Shall Be

Writers cannot write about the present. God does that. The present, thus, becomes the past before it can be born again from a writer's pen. But every page is a sign of hope in the future.

ECCLESIASTES **3:15**

That which is, already has been; that which is to be, already is; and God seeks out what has gone by.

Make Way for the Animals

When the writer Cleveland Amory died, his obituary took great notice of his love for animals. He was quoted as saying that if Paradise lacked animals, specifically cats, he wanted no part of it.

I hope, too, that Paradise has animals. In fact, it seems to me rather arrogant for humans to think that we alone among God's creatures will dwell in the house of the Lord forever.

Ecclesiastes 3:19

> For the fate of humans and the fate of animals is the same; as one dies, so dies the other. They all have the same breath, and humans have no advantage over the animals; for all is vanity.

TOM'S CATS

Tom is a layman who works in the bonsai shop of the monastery. He stops by every morning to check on his three cats who live in our barn.

Some mornings, when I am reading in the woods near the rear of the barn, I hear him speaking to them with touching tenderness and affection. They come to him because they know him and his goodness.

Tom's soft voice in the mornings gives me pause. I wonder about the ways to love that I have yet to learn—to love my enemies, to love those who hurt me, to love what seems dark and even evil, to love stray cats that I might easily ignore.

WISDOM 11:24

For you love all things that exist,
and detest none of the things
that you have made,
for you would not have made anything
if you had hated it.

WEARY WORKERS

My friend Mike, a teacher in Pennsylvania, is also a poet. He wrote a poem about the factory workers in the mill town where he grew up—men and women whose lives revolved around the tediousness of their work and the blowing of the factory whistle.

I was very moved by the words of the poem. I do not pass a factory now without thinking of Mike's weary people and the sensitive heart that honored them.

MATTHEW **11:28**

"Come to me, all you that are weary and are carrying heavy burdens, and I will give you rest."

THE MAN IN THE NICHE

Every morning when I was living in Rome for a month, I passed a poor man, an American, who lived in a niche in a wall that once housed a fountain. On a return visit eight months later, I walked by the niche and there he was. He looked at me and said, "Where ya been, man?" I was surprised he'd remembered me. He explained, "I learn a lot just by staying in one place and keeping my eyes open."

This man would have made a good monk.

1 CORINTHIANS 15:58

Be steadfast, immovable, always excelling
in the work of the Lord, because you know
that in the Lord your labor is not in vain.

CONSOLATION

I asked how the man in the casket had died. I was not acquainted with the family at all and wanted to know a little bit about what happened to him. I learned he had never married and had lived with his three unmarried sisters.

"He had the same routine every night, Father," one of them told me in a hushed, reverential tone. "At three or so in the morning he would go to the bathroom and then flush the toilet. We always listened for the flush because then we knew that he was okay. But a few nights ago, instead of the toilet flushing we heard a terrible crash. He had the heart attack right in the bathroom and fell near the sink. He must have died right away. We were so relieved that when he fell he did not strike his head on the sink and hurt himself."

I listened to her, my eyes fixed on the lifeless body of her brother. I thought to myself that there are different degrees of being hurt.

ECCLESIASTES **3:4**

A time to weep, and a time to laugh.

Wall Street

When I worked in the Wall Street area of Manhattan many years ago, I would sometimes sit in a small park near the World Trade Center before taking the subway back to New Jersey. Thousands of people passed by every couple of minutes during rush hour, heading for the cavernous depths of the Trade Center where the subways awaited them.

If I stayed long enough, another crowd soon passed —but going in the opposite direction. These were the women who cleaned the offices at night. Thousands of women went by, many of them new immigrants to America, most of them very poor. They chatted and laughed with each other. They did not have the serious demeanor and seemingly blind determination that characterized the earlier crowd. Indeed, they seemed happier, possessed of a richer spirit and lightheartedness.

LUKE **6:20**

"Blessed are you who are poor,
    for yours is the kingdom of God."

Ask and You Shall Receive

Catholic Worker founder Dorothy Day, an agnostic who converted to Catholicism, prayed that she might be given guidance, that someone would enter her life and teach her the ways of the gospel. Then one day, with a knock at her door, a man named Peter Maurin arrived. He was to radically change the course of her life or, more accurately, inspire her to allow God to change her life.

At the right time a teacher will come, says Zen wisdom. Christians know that to be true, too.

John 16:14

"He will glorify me, because he will take what is mine and declare it to you."

A View from Beijing

I was on a visit to China and awoke early. I stood on the porch of my hotel room in Beijing, and far below me I saw thousands of workers arriving in the city on bikes—a line of bikes as far as the eye could see. I then observed a group of men and women in a park next to the hotel going through the ritual of Tai Chi. They were swaying and locking their bodies in gravity-defying poses, as if trying to stretch themselves beyond limitations.

Two variations of human movement: laboring and stretching. May our lives be a blend of both.

Colossians 3:23-24

Whatever your task, put yourselves into it, as done for the Lord and not for your masters, since you know that from the Lord you will receive the inheritance as your reward.

THE FIRST DAY

The sun is just coming up and I am sitting on the porch at the rear of our church. Just below me, beyond the wall, are the graves of brother monks who have gone to their rest, and in the distance I can see the still waters of the lake. It is the beginning of the first day of creation.

We may only have today. Take a breath this day, breath in some love, breath it out, again and again.

GENESIS 1:5

God called the light Day, and the darkness he called Night. And there was evening and there was morning, the first day.

WHILE WE ARE SLEEPING

God brings good and beauty out of all things, and often does so when we are least aware. It is a good thing to remember. And to sleep on.

GENESIS 2:21-22

So the LORD God caused a deep sleep to fall upon the man, and he slept; then he took one of his ribs and closed up its place with flesh. And the rib that the LORD God had taken from the man he made into a woman and brought her to the man.

PASSION

Find your passion. Let it pass through you. Feel its depths, let it fire your heart. Passion is living hope; it is faith ablaze with a sight of the unseen.

PSALM 29:7

The voice of the LORD flashes forth flames of fire.

The Opposite of Joy

The opposite of joy is fear. When I am not joyful, I try to remember to ask myself what I am afraid of. What is it that darkens the light I need to live by?

I can be sad and yet know joy at the same time. But fear freezes joy.

Fortunately, a bit of quiet with myself usually thaws things out and my joy returns, complete and almost as if it had never left.

JOHN 15:11

"I have said these things to you so that my joy may be in you, and that your joy may be complete."

Osmosis

An old couple lived near the monastery many years ago. They were poor, and the monks used to bring them food and clothing. One day, according to one of the monks who was here at the time, Dorothy Day, who was on a visit to the monastery, went with a monk to the old couple's house and brought them a Bible. The couple accepted it with gratitude.

When the monk returned days later, however, the couple told him that they could not read or write but had put the Bible beneath their pillow. Before going to bed each night they prayed that some of its wisdom would enter them as they slept.

I wonder what Dorothy Day would have thought of that!

WISDOM **6:12**

Wisdom is radiant and unfading
and she is easily discerned by
those who love her,
and is found by those who seek her.

On Fire

If all the desire that exists in the world at this second could be harnessed towards loving, we would perhaps understand the nature of the fire that confounded Moses in the burning bush. Our hearts can be of that same fire. Our hope is that we learn what to set aflame.

EXODUS 3:2

There the angel of the LORD appeared to him in a flame of fire out of a bush; he looked, and the bush was blazing, yet it was not consumed.

GOD TIME

A friend of mine needs time every morning to be at peace. She wakes and sits quietly for a while with a cup of coffee, and then she leaves for work. She arrives early, before anyone else, and savors a half hour of solitude before the day's work begins.

She would probably not put it this way, but that is her God time—a time to be alone in peace, to gather strength for the day.

Experiences of prayer are more abundant than are our names and times for them.

JOHN 14:27

"Peace I leave with you; my peace I give you. I do not give to you as the world gives. Do not let your hearts be troubled and do not be afraid."

Slip Sliding Away

Sometimes I slip into the delusion that life should be trouble free and that if I am not happy something is wrong with the planet.

Then I slide further by assuming that I can make the necessary corrections to right the world.

These slips and slides always make for a miserable day.

John **16:33**

"I have said this to you, so that in me you may have peace. In the world you face persecution. But take courage; I have conquered the world!"

Good Cheer

While I was in college, I worked summers at a brewery in Newark, New Jersey. I had a friendly, happy boss, who made it a joy to go to work. One night he asked me to clean a large machine that was quite grimy. I scrubbed my heart out, removing the muck from all the metal parts. I hoped that by doing a good job, I was somehow making his life easier. His cheerful ways sparked in me a desire to work hard and work well.

Genesis 1: 31

God saw everything that he had made, and indeed, it was very good.

Please Note

Not far from where I lived in New Jersey is an area called the Meadowlands. It is now the home of an enormous sports complex which boasts several large arenas. Surrounding the complex are the vast meadows—a large, swampy area that stretches for miles. There is a dizzying collection of animals, insects, and plants that thrive in the Meadowlands. In their own way, they overshadow the massive cement and glass structures that now rise above the swamp.

As often as I drove past the Meadowlands, I never once thought of its fecundity until I read a book on the Meadowlands ecology. Now I wonder what else I may be passing by each day without noticing.

Mark 13:37

"What I say to you I say to all: Keep awake."

Author's Perks

I recently read an essay that said it has been scientifically proven that writing as self-expression is therapeutic.

I wonder if this holds true for the Author of Life. Does God get something good out of each new life, each new leaf, each new birth of a star that the Word brings into being?

John 1:3-4

All things came into being through him, and without him not one thing came into being. What has come into being in him was life, and the life was the light of all people.

CLOSE ENOUGH

My dad was an accountant. He loved numbers. I, on the other hand, always had trouble with math. Dad tried to help me with my arithmetic homework. I would sit down next to him on the couch as he tried to explain the figures to me using a yellow pad and his Cross pen. One time, before he wrote down an answer, he asked me what it was. I told him what I thought, but I was one digit off. He was exasperated. "Well at least I was close," I said hopefully. "Close isn't good enough with numbers!" he exclaimed, sailing beyond exasperation to despair. But he stayed with me until I figured out the correct answer by myself.

I can still see his hand moving the pen across his pad, the lamp above his head, the pattern of flowers on the couch on which I sat so close to him.

I cherish the lesson given to me by my dad: that close is good enough when it comes to love.

1 PETER 4:8

Above all, maintain constant love for one another, for love covers a multitude of sins.

The Beginning Is No Place to Start

Writer Walker Percy would begin writing a novel by placing a character in a predicament. These first thoughts put to paper were not necessarily the beginning of the finished story. He would not know that until the process of writing revealed to him just where he was headed. So, he would work backwards or forwards, depending on how the narrative developed.

Creation is not linear. It takes place at different rates, at different times, and from different vantage points.

Romans 8:22

We know that the whole creation has been groaning in labor pains until now.

Making Contact

We were at the beach when a friend of mine lost her contact lens. It blew from her fingertip as she was trying to put it on her eye.

I hate it when people lose things they really need, so I started to search. I found the lens—I really did— amid all that sand. I brushed it off as best I could and gave it to her. She said it was a miracle.

I felt like God for a brief moment: finding what was lost; restoring sight to the blind; bringing joy to the forlorn.

Isaiah 55:9

For the heavens are higher than the earth,
   so are my ways higher than your
      ways
   and my thoughts than your thoughts.

SALVATION CAT

Yesterday I was sitting in the woods on the monastery grounds. It was late afternoon, and I was looking at nothing in particular. In the distance I could see a dirt road that winds around a lake. A cat came into view, trotting along at a rapid pace. It looked as if it was in a hurry to get home to share some news with its friends.

I thought to myself: that cat has a pretty good life; it knows where it is going and bounces along with a spring in its step as if it knows all about the good tidings of salvation.

I should be more like that cat.

Job 12:9

"Who among all these does not know that the hand of the LORD has done this?"

FRINGE BENEFITS

I desperately wanted to be a part of certain popular groups when I was growing up. I was never good at sports but tried out anyway, because it seemed to be the thing to do. I did not make any teams—not even the "farm" team. I felt on the fringe—even beyond the fringe. But I survived by hanging around with other "sport fringies."

So here I am in a Trappist monastery. Another farm team. Another fringe group out in left field waiting to catch high flies from the Almighty.

PSALM **146:8-9**

The LORD lifts up those who are bowed
      down;
   the LORD loves the righteous.
The LORD watches over the strangers;
      he upholds the orphan and the
        widow,
      but the way of the wicked he brings
        to ruin.

Holy Chores

One of my favorite Zen sayings is: "Enlightenment comes. Then there is laundry to do."

I makes me think about what is holy and what is not.

I guess it will all come out in the wash.

Genesis 2:3

God blessed the seventh day and hallowed it, because on it God rested from all the work that he had done in creation.

HARVEST

None of us knows the final fruits of our labor. But how a person can grasp beauty and express it in words, paint, music or dance—is a preview of the ultimate harvest.

JOHN 4:36

"The reaper is already receiving wages and is gathering fruit for eternal life, so that sower and reaper may rejoice together."

JACOB

Jacob and I worked together in a Manhattan brokerage firm twenty-five years ago. He was an Orthodox Jew and dressed accordingly: black hat and suit and tie. It was his first prolonged venture into the Diaspora, and he struggled to find his way amid so many new people and customs.

Jacob was a kind man. I do not recall specific conversations we had, but I do remember many of them being about religion. Time has absorbed our words. What remains for me is the memory of Jacob's kindness. Nonessentials fade away; what is essential leaves an indelible imprint.

JOHN 1:47

"Here is truly an Israelite in whom there is no deceit!"

THE JOY OF JOHNNY MAHR

Johnny Mahr and I were in fourth grade together. I haven't seen him in forty years. What I'll never forget about him is how he loved to sing. He sang music he heard on TV, like the theme song to Captain Video. He sang while on the playground. He sang chasing balls. He sang his way out of fights and sang his way into my memory.

Johnny taught me at an early age that a song goes a long way in lightening life. Maybe that's why I've always been in choirs. Singing reminds me of the joy of Johnny Mahr.

EXODUS 15:2

The LORD is my strength and my might
        and he has become my salvation;
this is my God, and I will praise him,
        my father's God, and I will exalt him.

On the Nature of Things

I studied Latin in college, and for one class we had to translate "On the Nature of Things" by Lucretius into near perfect English on the final exam. On the morning of the exam, way before dawn, two classmates and I sat in a car parked in the university lot and crammed paragraph after paragraph into our heads. It was so early we had to use flashlights. By exam time, we knew the necessary paragraphs by heart and wrote them out without having to once consult the Latin text!

Perhaps the nature of things has to do with getting the words right first and then trying to live out their meaning. This is certainly true with monastic vows, ordination, marriage and other promises we make and then try to keep.

PSALM **61:5**

For you, O God, have heard my
vows;
you have given me the heritage
of those who fear your name.

At the Car Wash

One of the greatest pleasures I had as a kid was riding through a car wash. I loved the sensation of being pulled through a suds-filled monsoon with swirling tentacles of evil clawing at the windows. I felt safe and secure behind the car windows, all the while mesmerized by the roar of cleansing power.

There are days now when I feel as if I am once again going through a car wash, only this time without the protection of the car's sturdy windows and frame. I trust that I am being ruthlessly scrubbed and polished and buffed so that I may come out sparkling clean at the other end, but sometimes it is not as much fun as it used to be.

Psalm 51:7

Purge me with hyssop, and I shall be
clean;
wash me, and I shall be whiter
than snow.

Runaway Love

Juanita and I were classmates in the fourth grade. She was black and I was white, and she used to smile at me from across the room. One day she came up to me on the playground, looked at me for a few seconds, kissed me, giggled, and ran away. When my family moved away later that year, she cried and told me she loved me.

I can still see Juanita's face and remember how she laughed and kissed me and ran. When I think of her now, I wonder how many times I have run away from love.

I know of no stronger desire than to love.

Proverbs 27:19

Just as water reflects the face,
    so one human heart reflects another.

LIFE CYCLE

There are two baby mourning doves outside our cloister. They are only a few weeks old and nestle near each other beneath a bush. Their mother is always nearby and brings them food and watches them. Soon the time will come for them to take flight. A cycle of birth, growth, and departure will be complete.

I like watching these little birds and thinking about how all of life reveals something of its mystery through their simple patterns of growth.

Where am I in my life cycle? At times I feel as if I have taken flight, while at other times I experience a development period. And sometimes I wonder whether I've even been hatched yet.

ECCLESIASTES 3:6-7

A time to seek, and a time to lose;
a time to keep, and a time to throw away;
a time to tear, and a time to sew;
a time to keep silence, and a time to speak.

Coming up Short

During the summers I attended college, I drove a beer truck, making deliveries to stores and bars. One day I misread the height of a bridge and took the top of the truck right off.

I called the brewery dispatcher and told him what had happened. He asked three questions: Where was I? Was the truck capable of movement? Was there more beer to be delivered?

I told him where I was and that, yes, the truck could move and that more deliveries needed to be made. He never asked me how I was.

I got over my depression and finished delivering the beer. I soaked up whatever sympathy I could from the looks of people as I drove by with no roof on my truck and no smile on my face.

Job 29:2
_____

> "O that I were as in the months of old,
> as in the days when God watched over
> me."

POINTED OBSERVATIONS

While in Ireland many years ago I had a brush with death. I was in the front seat of a van as my friend who was driving tried to pass a tractor that was hauling a hay cock—a conical pile of hay pierced with a huge pitchfork. Our van did not clear the last prong of the fork. I saw that the van was going to be skewered and with less than a heartbeat to spare jumped out of the way. The prong ripped into the front of the van and right through the seat where I had been a second earlier. The van was lifted into the air and hurled, along with the tractor, into a wall. Miraculously, no one was hurt.

Later that night, I looked at my chest and knew that save for a millisecond it would have had a large hole in it. I looked at my friend and said, "I could have been killed."

"It's a good thing that you have a habit of always missing the point," was his unsympathetic reply.

PROVERBS 12:25

Anxiety weighs down the human heart,
but a good word cheers it up.

On the Gnashing of Teeth

Many years ago, after I was first ordained, I was at the Jersey shore on a Sunday morning and needed to cash a check. Knowing exactly where I could find some money, I went to a nearby rectory, rang the doorbell, and a portly priest answered. Sure enough, I could see a group of men counting the collection money from the Sunday Masses in a room just behind him.

I introduced myself and asked the priest if he could cash my check. He said no and closed the door in my face. I gnashed my teeth and left.

Not long ago I read that that same parish was swindled out of $1.5 million by a man who had first approached the pastor for a loan. The pastor fell for the scam and gave the man all that money to invest.

I am a poor monk now. Bereft of checks. Maybe I should write to the priest and tell him that our door is always open if he wants to come in from the cold winds of the night and the harshness of swindlers. He can wail and gnash his teeth away here.

Joel 1:13

> Put on sackcloth and lament, you
> priests;
> wail, you ministers of the altar.
> Come, pass the night in sackcloth,
> you ministers of my God!

Look What I Found in the Psalms

The Psalms don't teach, they reveal. I sing my own revelation everyday, several times a day.

Happy as a lark. Angry as a hornet. Busy as a bee. Sly as a fox. Slow as a tortoise. Dumb as an ox. Docile as a sheep. Gentle as a lamb. Fierce as a lion. Wise as an owl. Quick as a bunny. Lazy as a dog.

Purple with rage. Green with envy. Yellow with sickness. Black with depression. Blue with the blues. Happy with the yellows. Red with shame. Bright with hope. As good as it gets and as bad as it gets.

All these metaphors are buried in the Psalms. It is like being given a map of myself.

Psalm 119:103

How sweet are your words to my taste,
    sweeter than honey to my mouth!

Daily Avowal

I love the line from Dag Hammarskjöld's diary, *Markings*: "For all that has been, yes. For all that will be, thanks."

Can one reach a point in life when these words can be said in a lasting and definitive way? I hope so. My experience has been an avowed yes on a good Monday and a rethinking of the whole affair the rest of the week.

1 Samuel 10:9

As he turned away to leave Samuel, God gave him another heart; and all these signs were fulfilled that day.

My Best Self

I lie down in a hayfield. The blue sky above me. Tall grass all around me. Birds make their sure way across the sky. The sounds of insects fill the nearby woods. It is hot and humid. I am at peace.

I can do nothing here but be.

A sense of love rises from deep within me. It is my best self, and it is something greater than myself. This is who I am and who I want to be—even when I am far from this field.

This is who you are, too. Be still. Breathe deeply. Be your best self. And feel the love.

Ephesians 4:24

Clothe yourselves with the new self,
created according to the likeness of God
in true righteousness and holiness.

THE TRACES OF A KISS

There it was. A big kiss right at my feet on the floor of the abbey sanctuary. A woman had kissed the floor in reverence and her lipstick left the trace of a deep red, perfect smack. I stared at those rich red stains. The mark of love and desire, an expression of human longing, and the deeply erotic things we do with our lips to express our hearts.

I hope passionate people continue to grace our sanctuaries with kisses. We need love more than rules. We need love more than sacrifices. If there is to be a church in the next millennium, it will be one born of love, passion, and a refusal to have such denied.

PROVERBS **24:26**

> One who gives an honest answer
> gives a kiss on the lips.

Are We There Yet?

The ride from Atlanta to New Orleans is eight hours. I have driven it many times over the years. On one trip, my sister Mary and my niece Molly came with me. Molly was then three years old. We pulled out of the driveway, and when I stopped to make a turn at the end of the street Molly asked, "Are we there yet?" It was the first of perhaps eighty times that she would ask that same question. The miles passed. The question would not rest. Exasperated, I asked my sister whether Molly had any idea how long eight hours is. Mary looked at me and said, "Jeff, she is only three years old. Learning about time takes time."

When we pulled into Mom and Dad's driveway, I said "Molly, we are here." No answer. She had fallen asleep.

Romans **8:24-25**

For in hope we were saved. Now hope that is seen is not hope. For who hopes for what is seen? But if we hope for what we do not see, we wait for it with patience.

Brother Tom

Brother Tom takes care of the monastery garage and cars. When I owned a car, it looked as if I lived in it. When it came time to sell it, I had to clean it out and was amazed at what I found—it was like going on an archaeological dig.

Tom keeps the cars spotless. The insides are always clean and shiny. The windows glisten. Just the right amount of air freshener keeps the cars smelling new. He keeps a steady watch on oil and water levels. And if something goes wrong, he is all too happy to help. In short, he loves his work.

When I sit in one of our cars and put the key in the ignition, I think of Tom and the true meaning of labor: all things done with joy and care for others.

Philippians 1:22

If I am to live in the flesh, that means fruitful labor for me.

Laughter on a Summer's Eve

On warm summer evenings in Newark, New Jersey, I used to sit on the steps of the rectory and watch the life on the street. Of all the sounds of those nights, laughter coming through open windows was the best. It seemed the perfect background music to any lovely summer evening.

The laughter buoyed my spirits. Something inside of me felt connected to the people having a good time. I remember being glad that life, at least on those nights, was good for my neighbors. I would quietly wish them the genuine peace that should be near the hearts of those who laugh.

Psalm 126:2

Then our mouth was filled with
    laughter,
      and our tongue with shouts of joy;
then it was said among the nations,
      "The Lord has done great things for
      them."

The Voice of Nature

Nature is the keeper of my past. Sitting before a log fire, walking along the shore at night, or listening to the wind rustle through the trees evoke countless memories. It is as if a voice comes out of the fire, water, and wind and calls to long-forgotten pieces of my life and awakens them.

Why do I find this voice so compelling and what am I being asked to remember?

Judith 16:14

Let all your creatures serve you,
    for you spoke, and they were made.
You sent forth your spirit, and it formed
    them;
    there is none that can resist your
      voice.

LEAD KINDLY LIGHT

I have a family photograph that was taken in the living room of the house where I grew up. Mom and Dad are in the center flanked by my four brothers and two sisters, Grandma, and me. We're all clean and polished, smiling broadly for the camera. So many years lie ahead of each of us. Those years, as I now know them, have brought many things: marriages, births, deaths, good times and bad.

A light shines through the living room window.

God was there, sustaining our lives, hidden in the mystery of our hearts, our years, our living room.

The same light shines through the abbey church. It falls gently on all I see—still full of potential and hidden in mystery.

ISAIAH **60:19**

The sun shall no longer be
　　　your light by day,
nor for brightness shall the moon
　　　give light to you by night;
but the LORD will be your everlasting
　　　　　light,
　　　and your God will be your glory.

CROSSING THE STREETS OF LIFE

When I was little, Mom used to take me by the hand and walk me across the street. I can still feel the press of her hand.

I am older now but still as vulnerable as I was back then. At times, things come at me fast and furiously. I try to hold onto God's hand now. It feels like my mom's.

PSALM **37:23**

Our steps are made firm by the LORD,
when he delights in our way.

GEORGIA HEAT

The years may indeed fly by, but the heat of a summer day in Georgia can make an hour crawl to a near stop. The heat tempts me to wish for other times and places—for the cool of a Vermont winter or a breezy Jersey shore beach. But then the monastery is blessed with a late afternoon shower and the air becomes cool and refreshing. Glistening trees and grasses turn a deeper green. Birds bathe in the large puddles. And when the sun again shines, it is somehow with less intensity.

If I may liken divine life to the experience of a summer's day in Georgia, God is the relief that comes with the rain. Through torrents of love, God replenishes us and restores our souls.

SIRACH **43:22**

A mist quickly heals all things;
the falling dew gives refreshment
from the heat.

Name Dropping

I once wrote a short essay on Anne, who works in our retreat house. She is a wonderful, giving, humble woman. I put my heart into that piece. In my writing, I tried to do what Anne does for me and for all who are fortunate to know her: make the world a little better place.

I showed Anne the article. She was pleased but said she would prefer if I didn't publish it. I thought for a minute and struck a deal with Anne. If I changed her name would it be okay to publish the piece? She smiled and said yes.

I changed Anne to Ann.

James 4:6
_____

> "God opposes the proud,
>   but gives grace to the humble."

High Seas Adventure

Returning from a European trip many years ago, we were two days out of Southhampton, England on the Queen Elizabeth II. It was early morning, and I awoke to the sound of bells and the smell of smoke. When I put my feet on the floor, I felt heat.

There had been an explosion several decks below. We were all soon at our lifeboat stations. What a drama! Within hours everything was brought under control, however, and we never did have to abandon ship.

But we had to sail back to England for repairs. When we arrived in Southhampton, I called my pastor to tell him that I would be delayed coming back to the States. The answering machine at the rectory came on and listed the times for bingo that night. I tried again later and got the same tape. I finally left a message that all was well but that I would be several weeks delayed.

The QE II still sails the high seas. The parish still has bingo. The tape still plays. And I'm still alive. I passed through the mighty waters.

PSALM 32:6

Therefore let all who are faithful
offer prayer to you;
at a time of distress, the rush
of mighty waters
shall not reach them.

THE ICE CREAM MAN

When I was a kid, the ice cream man would come every afternoon in his white truck with bells ringing to announce his arrival. Even if I had no money, which was more often than not, it was a pleasure to wait for the truck and join the other kids when the ice cream man stopped at our corner.

The truck had thick doors with shiny handles like a moving treasure chest. Smoke-like frost would stream with a whoosh from each small door when it was opened. Just as quickly, the frosty air would disappear when the door was slammed shut.

The ice cream man wore a silver change maker on his belt and made change without ever looking. Coins spilled into his left hand as he pressed the small levers with the fingers of his right hand.

In minutes our business would be transacted and off he'd go down the street with bells ringing. We'd sit on the curb, enjoying our raspberry and orange popsicles, dixie cups, or ice cream sandwiches.

What a marvelous exchange. For a few coins so much was delivered.

SIRACH **51:27**

See with your own eyes that I have
labored but little
and found for myself much serenity.

SPEAK THE TRUTH

Word meanings change from time to time, from culture to culture, from person to person.

But God speaks in universal truths to all people at all times. Beauty, goodness, hope, love: to be human is know the what these words mean—even before we are moved to speak them.

JOHN **16:13**

"When the Spirit of truth comes, he will guide you into all the truth; for he will not speak on his own, but will speak whatever he hears, and he will declare to you the things that are to come."

THE FRAGMENTS OF LIFE

The thirty-four-year-old nephew of Damian, one of our monks, was killed recently when a tree limb fell on top of him and two others as they were sitting at a backyard gathering. The nephew had a young daughter, and his grieving wife does not know how the two of them will be able to cope. I can feel the woman's pain, even though I don't know her and she is many miles away.

This morning I watched another of our monks consuming the remaining pieces of Eucharist off the paten at Mass. He was very careful about those fragments. He put each one into his mouth with prayerful reverence.

There are times in life, sometimes very painful times, when we have to pick up the pieces, swallow them, and move on with our lives. In some strange way, the fragments of life are to be received with hope and reverence and, above all, the comfort of the love of others.

JOHN 6:12

> When they were satisfied, he told his disciples, "Gather up the fragments left over, so that nothing may be lost."

When Nature Is at Peace

I watch for deer in the early evening. These peaceful animals have an instinctive fear of humans. When I approach them, they dart away into the woods that border the monastery's large fields.

Will there come a time when such creatures approach us with curiosity and delight? On that day, I will know that the reign of God is at hand.

Isaiah **65:25**

The wolf and the lamb shall feed
    together,
    the lion shall eat straw like the ox;
    but the serpent—its food shall be
    dust!
They shall not hurt or destroy
    on all my holy mountain.

Sing Your Heart Out

On mornings when I wake up in the cloister feeling heavyhearted, I try to chant the Psalms with full feeling. Singing with soul helps chase away the blues. By the time the hour of Vigils is over, my burden is lifted and my heart is light again.

My hope is that everyone finds a place to sing their songs of joy each morning—be it a church, a shower, a car, or a under a tree in the park.

Psalm 40:3

He put a new song in my mouth,
a song of praise to our God.

Praying Geese

The first words we monks hear every morning at four are "O Lord, open my lips." These words are chanted by a different cantor each week.

Often, the geese down by the lake start honking immediately following the cantor's petition. The geese chorus is much louder than ours. Maybe God redirects our prayer requests every now and then.

Psalm 66:4

"All the earth worships you;
    they sing praises to you,
    sing praises to your name."

THE MAN IN THE BAR

I met a man in a bar and we started to chat. We got to talking about books and then hit the heavy philosophical theme of structuralism. We astounded each other by our familiarity with the topic. Big names flew from our lips: Derrida, Foucault, Levi-Strauss, Lacan, and other luminaries. We talked and talked and bought each other drinks and soon were as luminescent as the luminaries. I looked out the window. It was snowing. People passed by, talking and laughing as they walked. Suddenly I felt such love for all the words that have been written, sung, thought about, or said—words that touch upon who we are.

My friend and I parted ways, never to see each other again. I think of him every time I see a book by one of the authors we spoke of that night. We shared deep thoughts, and I will always remember him for that.

PSALM 4:7

You have put gladness in my heart
more than when their grain and
wine abound.

ZACHARY

Zachary is in fifth grade and the son of the publisher of this book. He and his dad visited the monastery a while back. There are not a lot of things for a fifth grader to do here, but we do have a golf cart. Zach wanted to drive, so off he and I went on a winding road that skirts a large field. It was difficult for him to get a feel for the gas pedal. He would either barely touch it or else he would floor it—giving the cart a hurky-jerky motion. He preferred to floor it, of course. He sailed over every bump with laughter and a sharp eye on the road ahead. The cart bounced along, giving much pleasure to its young driver and middle-aged passenger.

If Zach lives his years like he rode that day, he'll get to wherever he has to go with fleetness, precision, and—above all—joy.

ISAIAH **49:11**

And I will turn all my mountains into a
road,
and my highways shall be raised up.

GRAVE KEEPER

My friend Frank watches over my brother's grave.
He trims the hedges, pulls the weeds, keeps it
looking nice. His own brother is buried nearby.
Knowing Frank is one of the most enduring gifts of
my life. We each lost a brother and then grew as
close as brothers ourselves. When we see each
other again, we will share stories and laughter and
we will be completely ourselves—a sign of true
friendship. I think of that as I picture him pulling
weeds off my brother's grave.

PROVERBS **18:24**

Some friends play at friendship
but a true friend sticks closer than
one's nearest kin.

God's Emotions

Does God feel the same emotions we humans experience: anger, sorrow, joy, revenge, even hatred? If we are made in the divine image, then one would think that our feelings are shared by God. I hope that God is possessed of a heart that knows the storms and calms of our seas.

Genesis **6:6**

The LORD was sorry that he had made humankind on the earth, and it grieved him to his heart.

Inspired to Act

Sweet inspiration—it comes where the Spirit wills.
Be ready with your pen, your paint brush, your
heart, your voice. God is very generous.

Deuteronomy 31:22

That very day Moses wrote this song
and taught it to the Israelites.

Waiting with Frank

Several years ago, my sister called at two in the morning. Her son had been killed. It was the most painful conversation I have had in my life. Each word burned right through me. I hung up the phone and cried. I did not want to be alone so I called my friend Frank, who arrived at the rectory in minutes. He sat with me, just letting me be in my grief, a grief I know he shared.

Through Frank's friendship that night and many times since, I know something of the eternal comfort God promises each of us.

Genesis 28:15

"Know that I am with you and will keep you wherever you go, and will bring you back to this land; for I will not leave you until I have done what I have promised you."

THE DREAM

Last night I dreamed about my twin brother Jimmy, who died many years ago and whose name I took when I became a monk. In the dream he stood in my room here at the monastery, looking just as he had before he died. I asked if I could touch him. He smiled and took my hand and squeezed it with his own. His hand was warm. I asked him where Dad was, and he said that he was "around."

Everything seemed so real about Jimmy. When I awoke I wondered whether he had really been there in my room. Joy swept over me just knowing that he and my dad still exist in some manner I do not fully comprehend. I thank God for the hope of my dream. The dream is more real to me than my fears.

PSALM 16:7

I bless the LORD who gives me counsel;
in the night also my heart instructs me.

DAVID AT WORK AND AT REST

David, the brother of our prior, Brother Mark, is staying with us for a while. Lately, David has been working in a garden that he planted, picking squash, cucumbers, and tomatoes. I see him in the early evening, when it is cool, with a bandanna on his head and a big smile on his face as he goes about his work. He finds real pleasure in the things of the earth.

This morning I saw David sitting on a lawn chair way up on the fire escape of the retreat house. Right next to him was a potted palm, and he had a tiny table with a cup of coffee on it. He saw me, smiled, and waved.

At work and at rest, David seems peaceful and happy. Why can't we all be so?

1 SAMUEL **18:14**

David had success in all his undertakings;
for the LORD was with him.

Human Steps

I was in a bar in Elizabeth, New Jersey on the night the first man walked on the moon. My eyes were glued to the TV screen as Neil Armstrong took that first step. The people at the bar were silent. A feeling of awe and pride fell on the place. The bartender gave everyone a free round.

One of the patrons, who perhaps celebrated a bit too much, stumbled as he made his way out the door. "Good thing they did not send you to the moon!" someone guffawed. The place roared.

I smile when I think of the night I learned that no human step goes unnoticed.

Psalm 37:24

> Though we stumble, we shall not fall
> headlong,
> for the Lord holds us by the hand.

Nesting

I watched a mourning dove outside our cloister. She was picking twigs from the ground for a nest. She would select one, then discard it. She would then select another, and discard that one as well. On the third or even fourth try, she would find what she wanted and then fly away with the small piece of wood in her beak. Why that particular piece and not the others? Surely there was a reason. Her nest will be firm and intricately made—as fine a birthing place as our best hospitals.

Wisdom abounds in nature: simple wonders of which no living thing knows the source.

Days later I saw the nest. It was finely crafted. And her young will be even more so.

Job 28:20

"Where then does wisdom come from?
And where is the place of
understanding?
It is hidden from the eyes of all living,
and concealed from the birds
of the air."

MODERN GODS

I have both saluted different gods and given myself to them. What have been some of my gods been? Recognition? Money? Control? Pride?

The God we all need and ultimately seek is the God who moves the human heart to love and hope.

I pray that I have the wisdom and perseverance to follow that God.

ACTS 17:23

"For as I went through the city and looked carefully at the objects of your worship, I found among them an altar with the inscription, 'To an unknown god.' What therefore you worship as unknown, this I proclaim to you."

NEARER MY GOD TO THEE

On the twenty-fifth anniversary of my ordination, I had lunch with a small group of friends at the monastery. It felt good to be with them. For a quarter century, I have muddled my way through the high and low roads of religious life. How near am I to God? I have served in some beautiful churches, but I have never felt God's presence more than I did yesterday being with those dear friends.

ACTS **17:29**

"Since we are God's offspring, we ought not to think that the deity is like gold, or silver, or stone, an image formed by the art and imagination of mortals."

FACE TO FACE

As Jesus grew, his everyday discourse with others was as human as ours. From his conversations some important things were obviously revealed to him, but he apparently had no pressing need to write them down. Learning through speaking and hearing was enough for him.

Christianity is a face-to-face religion, God is revealed to each of us through others. Every face-to-face encounter can be a blessing, if we are ready to accept it.

3 JOHN 13-15

I have much to write to you, but I would rather not write with pen and ink; instead I hope to see you soon, and we will talk together face to face. Peace to you. The friends send you their greetings. Greet the friends there, each by name.

CENTERED LIVING

The ways of a child are self-serving. It is hard for him or her to be "other-centered." A child learns to be selfless from adults who show the way simply by living lives centered on others.

1 CORINTHIANS **13:11**

When I was a child, I spoke like a child, I thought like a child, I reasoned like a child; when I became an adult, I put an end to childish ways.

Magic Kingdom

A friend and I were arguing in a car on a South Jersey country road. As we sped along, the argument took as many turns as the wheels. Suddenly, as we rounded a bend, our eyes alighted on an enormous field scattered with hot air balloons. The sky was dotted with those that had already taken off. They were huge, colorful, majestic, and unlike anything I had ever seen before. It was as if we had driven into a magic kingdom. Our argument instantly deflated.

Psalm 104:1-3

> You are clothed with honor and
> majesty,
> wrapped in light as with a garment.
> You stretch out the heavens like a tent,
> you set the beams of your chambers
> on the waters,
> you make the clouds your chariot,
> you ride on the wings of the wind.

SORROWFUL MYSTERIES

Sorrow is as inevitable as it is painful. But it may be borne more tenderly if we trust that it is somehow God's sorrow, too. Jesus asks that we bear our sorrows with him and never apart from him. That is the sign of the cross.

MATTHEW **9:36**

When he saw the crowds, he had compassion for them, because they were harassed and helpless.

LABOR DAY PRAYER

Love what you do. Do what you love. Labor for justice.

PSALM 102:25

Long ago you laid the foundation
of the earth,
and the heavens are the work
of your hands.

Self-Help

We live in an age where self-help manuals, books, and workshops abound. My advice: concentrate on others and you will help yourself most.

1 Thessalonians 5:14

We urge you, beloved, to admonish the idlers, encourage the fainthearted, help the weak, be patient with all of them.

KEEP OUT!

When I was in fourth grade, all the boys formed a club called the Eagles. No girls were allowed. Everything was secret—oaths, meetings, pass-words, and the entrance of the clubhouse.

I wonder why we did that?

GENESIS 5:2

Male and female he created them, and he blessed them and named them "Humankind" when they were created.

TEMPORARY BLESSING

A woman asked that I bless her brand new car. She pulled it in front of the rectory and then stood there as I said the blessing and sprinkled it with holy water. She thanked me, drove out of the parking lot, and immediately crashed into a parked car.

Certain blessings have a limited shelf life, I guess.

LEVITICUS 25:21

I will order my blessing for you in the sixth year, so that it will yield a crop for three years.

Peace Restored

A woman drove hundreds of miles to the monastery for a few days of retreat and peace. On the day of her departure, she couldn't find her car keys. It was a rental car and all sorts of potential problems started to worry her. After a long search, she eventually found the keys and went on her way, greatly relieved and at peace once again.

Where, I wonder, do I mislay my peace on any given day? And what good does my worrying about it do?

2 Peter 3:14

Therefore, beloved, while you are waiting for these things, strive to be found by him at peace, without spot or blemish.

Strangers on a Plane

One time, my flight from Chicago to Newark was cancelled due to heavy snow. I did not mind. I had no special plans. The airline put us up in a hotel, and I had a nice dinner with several other passengers. We started out as strangers, but as the meal progressed we got to know each other a bit. That was thirty years ago. I can still see their faces and recall what they did for a living. I am glad we each made room for a stranger.

Ephesians 2:19

So then you are no longer strangers and aliens, but you are citizens with the saints and also members of the household of God.

TO BE LOVED

Youth is wondrous: to run in a field and fall in the grass, laughing and out of breath, and then to get up and run again; to know a summer night that seems to have no end; to experience the rush of first friends.

Youth is a time to learn how to love, but as one grows older it is more important to learn how to be loved: to be vulnerable and tender enough to be cared for, cherished, and even carried when necessary. We all reach a point when we can no longer run and perhaps cannot even breathe as we did in our youth. Then life beckons us to live from the love, the arms, the very breath of those who need to love us.

JOHN 21:18

Very truly, I tell you, when you were younger, you used to fasten your own belt and to go wherever you wished. But when you grow old, you will stretch out your hands, and someone else will fasten a belt around you.

SALVATION

How long it has taken me to learn that my salvation happens only when I let go of it?

MARK **10:26**

They were greatly astounded and said to one another, "Then who can be saved?"

HARSH REALITIES

I watched the kids playing in the schoolyard from the rectory window. A group of boys circled around one boy who was overweight, wore glasses, and looked awkward for his age. One of the boys hit him, and he went down. By the time I got to them, they had knocked his glasses off and smashed them to pieces. I broke the fight up and brought the boy into the rectory. He was crying. What was left of his glasses was in his hand.

He told me that he was not crying because of the kicks and punches but because he did not understand why the other boys had hurt him. I hugged him and felt tears in my eyes. I had no answer for him, and I still don't.

ISAIAH 53:7

He was oppressed, and he was
        afflicted,
    yet he did not open his mouth;
like a lamb that is led to the slaughter,
    and like a sheep that before its
        shearers is silent,
    so he did not open his mouth.

Death at Sea

A man swam out too far into the ocean, and soon he could no longer be seen. Lifeguards rushed into the water, diving frantically to find him. Finally the man's body was tossed onto the beach by the waves. He was dead.

There must have been a thousand of us on the beach that day, yet not a sound could be heard, save for the waves. As a crowd we moved as one, feeling the loss of something deep within us.

Slowly, as if emerging from a bad dream, people encircled the dead man's wife and embraced her. She wept. Her husband's lifeless body lay at her feet. Hundreds of strangers offered her whatever love and comfort they had within them. I was overwhelmed by our need for God.

John **6:16-17**

When evening came, his disciples went down to the sea, got into a boat, and started across the sea to Capernaum. It was now dark, and Jesus had not yet come to them.

How Does It Feel?

Three monks—Eutropius, Francis Michael and I—were standing in the driveway of our family guest house when over the radio from a nearby car came Bob Dylan's "Like a Rolling Stone." We started wailing the words. We knew them all: "How does it feeellll? To be on your own, a complete unknown, with no direction home?" We sang right along with Dylan—never missing a beat.

It was one of those rare times when the words to a song are especially pertinent. We monks know how it feels.

Mark 6:7-9

He called the twelve and began to send them out two by two, and gave them authority over the unclean spirits. He ordered them to take nothing for their journey except a staff; no bread, no bag, no money in their belts; but to wear sandals and not to put on two tunics.

Operator Assistance

When my first nephew was born, an operator was still needed to make long-distance calls. The woman must have waited on the line when the connection went through, and she heard our joy at the good news of the new arrival. I no sooner wished my sister Mary, her husband Brian, and their newborn baby well when the operator cut in and said that she just had to send her best wishes. I remember with fondness the operator's breach of protocol. I hope she did it often.

James 2:8

You do well if you really fulfill the royal law according to the scripture, "You shall love your neighbor as yourself."

Good Years

When my twin brother Jimmy died, my dad told me that we could move away if we thought that would help us deal with the pain. He thought that a new place, new people, new everything would possibly help. I told him that it would be better to stay, and so we remained in the place I have grown to love as my hometown.

I know my dad would have done anything to help the family heal our loss. But the ache was in us, and that would have moved with us, too. I think he was glad that we stayed. They were good years, years that matured us through our loss and brought us to a deeper kind of loving.

Luke 13:19

> "It is like a mustard seed that someone took and sowed in the garden; it grew and became a tree, and the birds of the air made nests in its branches."

THE GRAY PSALMS

I thought ours was to be a lasting friendship, but it abruptly and painfully ended when two people I cared about stole from me and then lied about it. There was no way I could recover what was lost—neither my valuables nor the friendship.

There are lines in our Psalter here at the monastery that are printed in gray, not black, which means we pass over them. The gray lines include the terrible psalms of a vengeful, almost hateful God.

Sometimes, however, I cheat and hum these "gray psalms" to myself. I confess that they are easily connected in my mind to that hurt I still feel about getting ripped off by "friends."

One day, the monk next to me at morning prayer surprised me when he whispered, "Here comes my favorite," as we approached one of the most horrific gray lines. I guess he must have gotten his ticket punched one time, too.

Vengeance may well be the Lord's, but every now and then it feels good to borrow just a bit of it.

ROMANS 12:19

Beloved, never avenge yourselves, but leave room for the wrath of God; for it is written, "Vengeance is mine, I will repay, says the Lord."

Marriage

A rabbi told a couple on their wedding day that love and the human heart were delicate. "But," he said, "God delights in delicacies. Leave room for him in your years and the gift of love will ripen."

Tobit **8:7-9**

"I now am taking this kinswoman of
    mine,
    not because of lust,
    but with sincerity.
Grant that she and I may find mercy
    and that we may grow old together."

Come Ye Apart

There is a bench on a corner in Bloomfield, New Jersey with the words, "Come Ye Apart and Rest a While" chiseled on it. The bench is v-shaped with room for just two people, who have to sit with their backs to each other, looking outward. That is one way to come apart and rest.

I've chosen another.

Genesis 2:2

On the seventh day God finished the work that he had done, and he rested on the seventh day from all the work that he had done.

Foot-in-Mouth Disease

My mom tells me that my twin Jimmy and I used to bite our toenails as little kids. (Not each other's. Apparently, we did have certain boundaries.) I have a vague recollection of doing this, but for the most part I have repressed this particular memory.

Mom says she never made us stop. There just came a day when Jimmy and I put our toes in our mouths for the last time. There was no struggle, no twelve stepping—just cold-turkey no-toeing.

Maybe a lot of my other bad habits will one day fall by the wayside. But until then, I have to take responsibility for the more advanced varieties of my foot-in-mouth disease.

Sirach 23:14

> Remember your father and mother
>   when you sit among the great,
> or you may forget yourself in their
>   presence,
>   and behave like a fool through bad
>   habit;
> then you will wish that you had never
>   been born,
>   and you will curse the day of your
>   birth.

THE WAY OF LOVE

I watch Chaminade, one of our monks, care for our old and sick monks with ease and joy. The more he gives, the happier he is. Often, he is the memory, eyes, hands, and feet of those who are now weak. Watching Chaminade is a lesson in the way of God and of our Trappist life.

SIRACH **3:12-13**

My child, help your father in his
old age,
and do not grieve him as long
as he lives;
even if his mind fails, be patient with
him;
because you have all your faculties
do not despise him.

The Main Course

Beattie was the cook in my last parish. Microwave ovens baffled her. I would hear the high ping of the "ready" signal and then a mumble from Beattie as she discovered that the food was not heated to her liking. So out would come the pots and pans, and soon she would be making soup—something she did to perfection. Beattie knew to pursue a course she could master.

Sɪʀᴀᴄʜ **3:23**

Do not meddle in matters that
are beyond you,
for more than you can understand
has been shown you.

Good Morning

Damian is a happy monk. He has two dogs, Bozo and Sasso, whose home is the large garage where Damian's tools are kept. When I sit in the woods early in the morning, I hear Damian greet the dogs. They hear him coming and welcome him with whines and barks and scratchings on the large wooden door. He talks to them as he approaches, lets them out, pets them, and feeds them. I watch and listen to it all, and know that I am in the presence of Wisdom.

SIRACH **4:11-12**

Wisdom teaches her children
and gives help to those who
seek her.
Whoever loves her loves life,
and those who seek her from
early morning are filled with joy.

ONE ROAD

To make a choice is to trust a path and stick to it.
There are times when I get tired and think another
way might be better. There are times when I look
at the others on a path near mine and get envious,
for they look happier than I. There are times when
I cannot see ahead of me and want to go back
and retrace my steps.

Yet sometimes I see others on those near paths
looking at me. Then I know that we all walk the
same road.

SIRACH 5:9

> Do not winnow in every wind,
> or follow every path.

SACRED FRIENDSHIP

I have friends who have been with me for a long time. I dream of them, hope for them, and am grateful for them. They are gifts that I do not possess but do not worry about losing, either. For when I look into my very self, I realize they are a part of me. They are with me despite any kind of absence. I cannot be who I am without them. Friendship is something of a sacrament—my friendships have become part of my very flesh and spirit.

SIRACH **6:14**

Faithful friends are a sturdy shelter:
whoever finds one has found a
treasure.

Humble Tommy

Tommy was an Irish farmer who never married and lived his entire life on his small sheep farm in County Mayo, Ireland. His house was rustic and austere. He sat by the fire at night, smoking his pipe and listening to his little radio. When he spoke, his words were carefully chosen. When he listened, he did so with attentiveness, as if every utterance were a treasure. His world was as small as his farm, for he rarely ventured far from it. But he was at home with stillness, with solitude, with very simple pleasures. I believe he realized more monastic aspirations than I ever will.

Sirach 3:20

For great is the might of the Lord;
but by the humble he is glorified.

THE GREATEST OF THESE

A reckless young man veered off a country road and unintentionally drove into a group of Amish children, killing several of them. I read that the father of one of the children publicly forgave the young man.

A poll for Person of the Century is currently being conducted. Many familiar names have made the top-one-hundred list—people who have made great contributions in peace, science, business, and the arts and letters.

That father has my vote.

PSALM 62:11-12

Once God has spoken;
     twice have I heard this:
that power belongs to God,
     and steadfast love belongs to you,
       O Lord.

SAVED FROM RUIN

My kindergarten teacher, Miss Temple, laid the foundation for the many times in my life I have been rescued from disaster. One day she told the class to build a house out of large, red foam blocks. As I performed our handiwork from the inside, some kid pushed the house from the outside and it fell in on me. I was buried beneath a mound of foam.

Miss Temple dug me out and scolded the mini-Terminator. She taught me that all human constructs are faulty and that it's up to each of us to come to one another's aid.

1 KINGS 9:8

"This house will become a heap of ruins; everyone passing by it will be astonished, and will hiss; and they will say, 'Why has the LORD done such a thing to this land and to this house?' "

SHARP CONTRASTS

People come in a wide variety—different shades of color, height, shape, proportion, gait. A simple gaze can easily detect startling contrasts among the individuals in any group of citizens.

The contrasts among people that Jesus brought into sharp relief, however, were of human making—rich and poor; privileged and oppressed; free and slave; hard-hearted and merciful. His observations have been afflicting the comfortable and comforting the afflicted for two millennia.

LUKE 21:1-2

He looked up and saw rich people putting their gifts into the treasury; he also saw a poor widow put in two small copper coins.

The Smell of Wisdom

Many years ago, a young boy confessed to me that he had made fun of a kid who smelled of garlic. I did not ask any questions, gave him his penance, and told him he was forgiven.

Several weeks later another boy came into the confessional, reeking of garlic. I asked him if he had eaten garlic, and he said that he did so all the time. I asked whether his friends ever made fun of him. He said they did but that he loved garlic. I told him that he had a choice to make between garlic and friends.

Eventually, friends won out. Sometimes, wisdom is pretty easy to sniff out.

2 Corinthians 2:15-16

For we are the aroma of Christ to God among those who are being saved and among those who are perishing; to the one a fragrance from death to death, to the other a fragrance from life to life. Who is sufficient for these things?

Surf's Up

One day, after a very heavy storm, I went for a walk around the monastery grounds and stopped by a bridge. A creek, normally very serene, roared below. I saw a beaver riding the waters on his back. When he saw me, he turned on his belly and kept right on going. He seemed delighted to be carried along. Maybe he was surfing home.

The Word of God carries us like that. We are sustained by the Good News, our spirits rise, and we ride high all the way home.

James 1:22

Be doers of the word, and not merely hearers.

Patterns of Listening

Catherine was a seamstress I knew many years ago. She had a thorough knowledge of countless fabrics, patterns, buttons, colors, and weaves. Her apartment was filled with bolts and cuts of cloth, and the clothes she made were beautiful.

I once asked her how she knew so much. She loved to sew, she said, from the time she was a little girl. She watched and listened to her mother and grandmother and patterned herself after them.

Sirach 6:33

If you love to listen you will gain
knowledge,
and if you pay attention you
will become wise.

Reprieve

When we were young, my brother Johnny was never good at being direct. He had a pesky acquaintance who lived up the street, and one day he spotted the annoying neighbor making his way toward our front door for a visit. Johnny took the most expeditious action he could think of—he opened a back window, jumped out, and ran away for several hours.

Eventually, all of us have to face what we find disconcerting. But sometimes temporary exile is in order.

Exodus 2:15

When Pharaoh heard of it, he sought to kill Moses. But Moses fled from Pharaoh. He settled in the land of Midian, and sat down by a well.

PRIME MOVER

Sitting in a restaurant by myself in a New Orleans hotel several years ago, I gazed out at the Mississippi River. Large ships slowly made their way up its muddy waters. The lights of the Crescent City twinkled. The sun was setting. So much movement, I thought, taking place all over the world at that moment. Does the divine spirit move within it all, gently but surely bringing it all to itself? Yes, I thought, God is in the river, in all waters, in all things, in me—looking for a lasting port.

Those who enter God's rest also cease
from their labors as God did from his.

A Simple Life

The world was astonished at the discovery of the body of a man who had been frozen in a glacier for thousands of years. He apparently died with what few possessions he had: basic clothing, a pouch for his tools, a cape for cold weather. His simple life was commented upon with envy in many newspaper articles. To go through life with few possessions is a grace.

1 Timothy 6:6-8

Of course, there is great gain in godliness combined with contentment; for we brought nothing into the world, so that we can take nothing out of it; but if we have food and clothing, we will be content with these.

BLOOD BROTHERS

My friend Bobby and I became blood brothers in third grade. We must have seen the ritual in a Western movie. We cut our fingers just a bit and placed them on top of each other so that our blood commingled. We then promised friendship for life. If need be, we would die for each other. It all felt so glorious.

Adult vows should be made with as much conviction and passion. I hope my long-lost blood brother has found someone or something worth living and dying for.

PHILIPPIANS 1:29

> He has graciously granted you the
> privilege not only of believing in
> Christ, but of suffering for him as well.

Passing Storms

Earlier this morning at the monastery, the skies darkened and the heavens opened. The storm was fierce. Thunder shook the roof of the shed where I was sitting, and lightning smacked and hissed at very close range.

Within an hour the skies were clear and the sun was shining. The rest of the day was beautiful.

Life's storms pass, too.

Psalm 57:1

Be merciful to me, O God, be merciful
to me,
for in you my soul takes refuge;
in the shadow of your wings I will
take refuge,
until the destroying storms pass by.

ANGELA'S PRAYERS

Angela arrives very early every morning at the small church in North Jersey where I served for seven years. Sometimes I would go into the sacristy, well before dawn, and hear her saying her prayers as she moved from one statue to the next. She prayed for those she loved and for those she would never meet. Hearing her would jolt me into realizing that life lived for others does not necessarily involve hands-on doing for them. There are times when our best action toward another is prayer.

I think of Angela when I awake early in the morning at the monastery. I am grateful for what she taught me. I pray for her as she prays for countless others.

EPHESIANS 1:16

I do not cease to give thanks for you as I remember you in my prayers.

Why Did God Make Me?

In first grade, I memorized the catechism that I was made "to know, love, and serve God." After years of reading, searching, questioning, studying, I don't believe I've come up with a better answer to why God made me than what I learned when I was seven.

Ephesians 3:18-19

I pray that you may have the power to comprehend, with all the saints, what is the breadth and length and height and depth, and to know the love of Christ that surpasses knowledge, so that you may be filled with all the fullness of God.

LEAVING HOME

Yesterday I was walking in the cloister and saw a baby bird, still covered with soft down, right in the middle of a path. He looked frightened, bewildered, and stranded. His mother was nearby and squawked at my presence. Apparently she was teaching him how to live on his own outside the nest.

Some things we can learn only by leaving home.

PROVERBS 27:8

Like a bird that strays from its nest
is one who strays from home.

LIFE-AND-DEATH MATTERS

If we could make peace with loss, with death, with being finite, our day-to-day living would be more joyful. In Christ, life and death are inseparable. There cannot be one without the other.

What comes from death? The loss of a grudge, the birth of a new day, the dying to oneself, the rising to new life.

PHILIPPIANS 1:21

For to me, living is Christ and dying is gain.

GATHERING TIME

A fellow monk used to walk into the room where I liked to spend my mornings and shout a good-natured greeting at the top of his lungs. He would then chatter on about everything under the still-rising sun. He apparently had no need for quiet "gathering time" in the morning. I did, so I gathered my thoughts and started spending my mornings elsewhere. We found our separate peace.

JAMES 5:8-9

Strengthen your hearts, for the coming of the Lord is near. Beloved, do not grumble against one another, so that you may not be judged.

FALSE WITNESS

When I moved to a new parish one time, a particular parishioner was freely bad-mouthed by fellow parishioners whenever the opportunity arose. When I finally met the man, however, I took an instant liking to him. He told me not to pay attention to all that was said about him.

As the years went on, I could see why the man avoided people; yet this merely fueled their suspicions of him. He had a girlfriend, and it was through her that I discovered what a good man he really was.

The slander that enveloped this man saddens me to this day. The person his detractors spoke of never existed.

WISDOM 1:11

Beware then of useless grumbling,
and keep your tongue from slander;
because no secret word is without
result,
and a lying mouth destroys the soul.

Simple Acts

A giant red ball of fire is setting in the west over the monastery lake. Deer graze not far from me. Kind things were said and done this day: Mom sent me a letter; an old monk made his way to the grave of one of our monks who died last week to make sure that the cross is situated just right.

God becomes known to us in these simple acts.

Romans 12:9-10

Let love be genuine, hate what is evil, hold fast to what is good; love one another with mutual affection; outdo one another in showing honor.

THE SURGEON

I once knew a brain surgeon who, having seen so much suffering in children, said he could not believe in a benevolent God. Still, the man went about his work his entire life with kindness and genuine peace. One day a week he worked in a clinic for no pay.

I very much admired this man who spent his life bringing to people something of the God in whom he had no faith.

LAMENTATIONS **2:11**

My eyes are spent with weeping;
   . my stomach churns;
my bile is poured out on the ground
      because of the destruction of my
            people,
because infants and babes faint
      in the streets of the city.

You're Better Than That

From the time we are young until the time of our deaths, those who love us will tell us when we have strayed from our best selves. Admonishing the sinner is a spiritual work of mercy.

1 Thessalonians 5:11

Encourage one another and build up each other, as indeed you are doing.

Dr. Myers' Hands

Dr. Myers was our family doctor when I was growing up. He wore a blue coat and carried a black leather bag when he made house calls. I remember his kindness, his laugh, and how he used to tap me on the knee with a little hammer to test my reflexes. But most of all I remember his hands, how they touched and healed and felt for signs of swelling and weakness.

Year's later, those same hands opened as I gave him and his wife Anne the Eucharist at my ordination. On other occasions, his hands held mine and those of my family when a loved one died. His hands now hold a pen when he writes me a letter or a phone when he calls my mom.

Through his two beautiful hands, Dr. Myers has found a way to touch my life and the lives of countless others.

Sirach **38:1-2**

Honor physicians for their services,
    for the Lord created them;
for their gift of healing comes from
        the Most High,
    and they are rewarded by the king.

MEAL PREPARATIONS

Mom and Grandma spent hours cooking dinners when I was growing up. Sundays meals were extra special. I believe Mom and Grandma had a picture in their minds of how each meal would turn out as they washed and cut the vegetables, prepared the roast, and made the dessert.

Jesus spoke more than once of a heavenly banquet, and we all have a vision of what it will be like. But now is the preparation time for the meal. It is good to keep the final feast in mind as we do the routine things of any given day. These tasks are a necessary part of what is to come and a real part of the joy that shall be given us when we sit down to a meal that shall never end.

HABAKKUK 2:3

For there is still a vision for the
appointed time;
it speaks of the end, and does not lie.
If it seems to tarry, wait for it;
it will surely come, it will not delay.

SPACE TRAVEL

My friends and I built rocket ships when we were kids. They did not go very far. We made them from large cardboard boxes. We cut out spaces for windows and made a cockpit with a control panel festooned with buttons made from soda bottle caps. For gauges we used meters from an old oven. The steering wheel was the wheel of an old bike. With a healthy dose of imagination, we blasted off and traveled the galaxy, leaving the reality of the basement far behind.

I still travel like that—only now it's from an old chair behind the monastery barn—my imagination spurred by turning the pages of books that send me into universes filled with love and hope.

ISAIAH **35:8**

A highway shall be there,
  and it shall be called the Holy Way;
the unclean shall not travel on it,
  but it shall be for God's people;
  no traveler, not even fools,
   shall go astray.

The Cry of Being

I heard a kitten crying in the barn, but when I spotted her she ran away. She was only a few weeks old and was abandoned by her mother. I left food and water for her, but she was frightened and scampered behind a large woodpile every time I approached.

I found her lifeless body one morning near the woodpile. I do not know what she died from. I picked her up and buried her behind the barn.

I still think of that kitten's cry when I sit down and read near the barn. I believe that if all living things had a single voice we would cry together for what we all need—the presence of God in our lives.

Joel 1:20

Even the wild animals cry to you
because the watercourses are
dried up,
and fire has devoured
the pastures of the wilderness.

Happiness

Every night at Compline, we monks chant, "What will bring us happiness, many say?" I think about all the things I have sought over the years to bring me happiness: money, relationships, a nice place to live, a good vacation, a villa in the Swiss Alps, front-row seats at a Bob Dylan concert, a cocktail with a Kennedy.

Here at the monastery happiness is not about having or getting. Rather, it has to do with listening, living, and being myself. Such happiness far outlasts the concerts, drinks, and exotic vacations.

Jonah 2:8

Those who worship vain idols
    forsake their true loyalty.

OVERPLANNING

At her wedding rehearsal, a bride-to-be told me that she wanted the statue of Mary moved from the back of the church to the front. I declined her request because the statue was too heavy. She pouted.

She wanted the front pew unscrewed and moved. I declined her request because it was against parish policy. She pouted.

She said that I was ruining her plans. I told her that if she made too many plans it would take away from the joy of her wedding.

The next day vows were exchanged; all went well; and off the couple went—past the statue of Mary and the pew that was not moved.

I later found out that the groom had a kidney stone attack at the reception. The honeymoon was delayed. So much for the bride's many plans.

JONAH 4:6-7

> The LORD God appointed a bush, and made it come up over Jonah, to give shade over his head, to save him from his discomfort; so Jonah was very happy about the bush. But when dawn came up the next day, God appointed a worm that attacked the bush, so that it withered.

WHO'S TO BLAME?

Those times—and there have been more than a few—when I've gotten myself into a real mess, my first reaction was to blame everybody and everything other than myself. I blamed the system, the culture, the powers that be, my parents, my teachers, the Pope, and anyone else I could drag into it...including God. But my woes were always the result of bad choices that I had freely made.

Amazingly, help in all these situations was also freely given by friends, family, the church, and anyone else who saw my need...most especially God.

MICAH 3:4

Then they will cry to the LORD,
       but he will not answer them;
he will hide his face from them at that time,
       because they have acted wickedly.

Please See the Waitress

He was sitting at a corner table in an airport restaurant. He was on the phone, laughing with the person on the other end of the line, his eyes darting about taking in his surroundings. Then I realized that he was not really focusing on anything. He was blind. The waitress came over and kidded him about missing some food on his plate. She arranged his eggs in a small pile, placed a fork in his hand, and moved his hand to the eggs. His face turned toward her, and he smiled, nodded, and then continued his chat on the phone.

How full of kindness the world is. My prayer is simply to see deeply and to take to heart the beauty that flows so wondrously from life, from the corners of restaurants, from the heart of a waitress.

Mark 10:51

> Then Jesus said to him, "What do you want me to do for you?" The blind man said to him, "My teacher, let me see again."

EARLY MASS

I used to love daily Mass in parish churches, especially the early Mass. There would be a delicate mix of old and young, the physically, mentally, and spiritually ill, oddballs and eccentrics, and just plain folks. I felt at home with my weaknesses and strengths, joys and sorrows. Without ever talking about it, we participants at these daily Masses supported one another and made God's presence felt.

1 CORINTHIANS 1:26

Consider your own call, brothers and sisters: not many of you were wise by human standards, not many were powerful, not many were of noble birth.

FIELD OF FAITH

While riding on a train in China many years ago, I looked out the window as we passed mile after mile of countryside—awed by the vastness of the land. The train slowed as it passed a field, and off in the distance beneath a cluster of trees I spied a man and woman bowing before a small statue with candles in front of it. They were obviously showing reverence to a reality or being beyond themselves. I recognized something of myself in that man and woman and their simple act of faith among such vast possibilities.

1 CORINTHIANS 2:1-2

> When I came to you, brothers and sisters, I did not come proclaiming the mystery of God to you in lofty words or wisdom. For I decided to know nothing among you except Jesus Christ, and him crucified.

SEARCH ME

Love is on a constant search for what is good and calls forth that goodness in myriad ways, across miles and years. Our greatest joys and fondest memories are the fruit of that search.

1 CORINTHIANS 2:9-10

As it is written,
> "What no eye has seen, nor ear
> heard,
> nor the human heart conceived,
> what God has prepared for those
> who love him"–
these things God has revealed to us
through the Spirit; for the Spirit searches
everything, even the depths of God.

UNMASKED

I have been a ghost, goblin, angel, devil, farmer, skeleton, pirate, and cowboy over the course of my youth on Halloween nights. While in costume, I distinctly sensed my inner and outer selves and the difference between them.

I no longer dress up and go trick-or-treating on October 31, yet I am still aware of different selves that I am—selves I wear like so many masks.

I look at the older monks here, however, and sense that they smile with a loving acceptance from having become their true selves. In their smiles I see patience and a silent encouragement. No masks, just the self.

EPHESIANS **4:25**

So then, putting away falsehood, let all of us speak the truth to our neighbors, for we are members of one another.

Saints Preserve Us

Once there was an earthquake near a small Italian village. Damage was extensive, but there was no loss of life.

The villagers were annoyed at their patron saint for not taking better care of them. A reporter saw a woman throw a statue of the saint onto the street. Then she slammed the door. The statue lay in pieces on the road.

It appears that even saints must keep up their good work.

James 2:15

Faith by itself, if it has no works, is dead.

On Earth as It Is in Heaven

From a distance, I watched a woman walking in the cemetery. She approached a grave and made the sign of the cross. She knelt and placed flowers in front of the headstone. Then she bowed and kissed the earth. Her lips touched all things human and all things divine. I found myself hoping that God kissed her back with as much love.

Wisdom 3:9

Those who trust in him will
        understand truth,
and the faithful will abide with him
        in love,
because grace and mercy are upon
        his holy ones,
and he watches over his elect.

The Power of Presence

There are times when we are confronted with the pain of another and cannot find the right words to offer. We Americans are a loquacious people and assume that every situation has a corresponding "right" thing to say.

But our presence means much more to suffering people than our words. Pain cannot be taken away by words. But the presence of another person does make times of trouble easier to bear.

JEREMIAH **8:21**

For the hurt of my poor people
I am hurt,
I mourn, and dismay has taken
hold of me.

LIMIT YOUR EXCESS

I once read an obituary in which the wife of the deceased, when asked what her relatively young husband had died from, replied, "Everything. He did it all."

Apparently, longevity requires learning to live within limits.

PROVERBS **19:2**

Desire without knowledge is not good,
and one who moves too hurriedly
misses the way.

POCKET-SIZED GIFT

I wear a medal that a friend gave to me as a gift a
long time ago. I am glad that she did not give me
something large that would have been difficult to
have with me at all times. Small gifts, given with
love, wear well.

GENESIS **32:13**

So he spent that night there, and from what
he had with him he took a present for his
brother Esau, two hundred female goats
and twenty male goats, two hundred ewes
and twenty rams, thirty milch camels and
their colts, forty cows and ten bulls, twenty
female donkeys and ten male donkeys.

For Clara

I once knew a poor couple who lived out of an old car. They somehow scraped together enough money to get by from day to day. I would see their car pull into the church parking lot and was always anxious to hear their rich stories of the road.

They cared as best they could for their grand-daughter Clara, whom they were raising. I eventually helped them cut through the red tape to get government benefits and an apartment.

I once asked them what kept them going. "Clara," replied the grandmother. "We will live and die for her. We don't have much, but we will give her all the love we have."

Clara, your cup runneth over.

Psalm 23:5-6

You anoint my head with oil;
  my cup overflows.
Surely goodness and mercy shall
    follow me
  all the days of my life,
and I shall dwell in the house of the
    Lord
  my whole life long.

Branching Out

I can see a tree from the window of the barn where I sit to write. Its branches have found their way up and through the metal bars of a fence, twisting them and bending them in the process. The tree and fence now belong together, an entwined blend of wood and metal. If the fence is taken down, the tree will die. If the tree dies, the fence—embedded in its trunk and branches—will fall when the tree falls.

So it is with God. We grow in and through the divine reality, until we become one with it.

John 15:5

"I am the vine, you are the branches.
Those who abide in me and I in them bear
much fruit, because apart from me you can
do nothing."

Heartening Words

Michael, one of our novices, recently left to enter another monastery far from here. He is a very easygoing person. I will miss him.

He left a note in my mailbox the morning he left, thanking me for encouraging him, especially on days when he had lost heart. He said that during his time with us he learned that the gift of heart is a shared gift. I smiled to myself when I read his note. I will keep it for a day when I, too, need encouragement. Michael can then share the gift of heart with me.

2 Corinthians 4:1
___

Therefore, since it is by God's mercy
that we are engaged in this ministry, we
do not lose heart.

Houses of God

One of my deepest senses of church comes to me when I help my fellow monk Chaminade care for the old and sick in the monastery's infirmary.

Magnificent cathedrals have been built and filled with treasures to the honor and glory of God. But an old soul making his or her way from this life to the next is no less beautiful. In their weakness and need, dying people are the most sublime temples on earth.

1 Corinthians **3:16**

Do you not know that you are God's
temple and that God's Spirit dwells in you?

Deliver Us, O Lord

The Psalms are filled with petitions to God for deliverance from every conceivable horror: murder, pestilence, hunger, abandonment, depravity, hell.

Yet the anguish that is the root of human suffering does not come from God. It is our own doing. In effect, we pray that we might be delivered from ourselves, from the pain we cause one another.

God is by no means silent. Our struggles to be loving each day are the divine response to our petitions. God delivers us through the very acts of love we perform.

Genesis 32:11

Deliver me, please, from the hand of my brother, from the hand of Esau, for I am afraid of him; he may come and kill us all, the mothers with the children.

THE LIGHT OF THE WORLD

I recently read that the vast darkness that stretches between the constellations of stars is some sort of strange matter so dense that it absorbs the light of all the other billions of stars.

The many faces we come across in our lives are like those stars. God's light shines through them all, but the light of some gets trapped in the density of our prejudices, resentments, or fading memories.

Someday, God's light will burst through, and like an enormous fire in the sky every shining star and glowing face will be seen in all its glory. God's love will transfigure the heavens and the earth.

ECCLESIASTES **8:1**

Who is like the wise man?
    And who knows the interpretation
      of a thing?
Wisdom makes one's face shine,
    and the hardness of one's counte-
      nance is changed.

A Very Important Guest

For any festive occasion we want to make sure
that those who mean the most to us are present.
People are consulted. Lists are drawn up and
pored over.

Don't forget to put the ultimate VIP on your list.

And, Lord God, the favor of a reply is requested.

Isaiah 54:7

For a brief moment I abandoned you,
but with great compassion I will
gather you.

WHAT MRS. ULRICH SEES

Mrs. Ulrich baby-sat for my family many years ago in New Jersey. She was rather plump, had a chirpy voice, and never took her hat off. "God sees every-thing," she told us. "But whatever God does *not* see, I *will* see." It worked. We rarely misbehaved.

I hope Mrs. Ulrich is in Paradise now, where she can kick off her shoes, take off her hat, and relax her vigilance.

PHILIPPIANS 2:12-13

Therefore, my beloved, just as you have always obeyed me, not only in my pres-ence, but much more now in my absence, work out your own salvation with fear and trembling; for it is God who is at work in you, enabling you both to will and to work for his good pleasure.

Behind the Scenes

When I was five years old, we lived on a lovely tree-lined street in Hempstead, Long Island. One day as I was walking past the house of a neigh-bor, I heard the wife shriek at her husband, "Do not forget that I rule you!" Even at five, I knew enough not to like the sound of that. I walked home fast.

Ephesians 5:21

Be subject to one another out of reverence for Christ.

Live and Let Live

Pee Wee and I work together in the monastery barn wrapping bonsai pots. One summer's day, he warned me that there was a wasp in our work area. I could hear it but could not see it. It then landed near Pee Wee's foot. He gently nudged it out the door, and the wasp flew off, leaving us unstung.

Witnessing Pee Wee's gentle action taught me a lesson about the Christian reverence for life—even that which can be harmful to us.

1 Peter 3:9

Do not repay evil for evil or abuse for abuse; but, on the contrary, repay with a blessing. It is for this that you were called–that you might inherit a blessing.

POETRY RECITAL

I once visited an elderly man in a nursing home who was struggling to adapt to his new life. His memory was fading, and he missed his old friends. We chatted for a bit and somehow got on the topic of cats. His face lit up, and he asked me whether I'd like to hear a poem. "Sure," I said. With that he recited line after line of a poem about cats. He went on for several minutes. I was amazed at how much he had committed to memory. When he was finished he sighed and said, "I love that poem. It is easy to remember things I love."

LUKE **23:42**

Then he said, "Jesus, remember me when you come into your kingdom."

THE POOR MAN

The man had lost his job and been out of work for a long time. I noticed that he kept his distance from his former friends, and one day I asked him what had happened between them.

"Without a job," he told me, "things change. When I get a job, they'll come around again."

He seemed to take this insight in stride. Yet as time went on I saw him less and less at parish gatherings. The lack of a steady income isolated him and his wife from the community. Eventually, they sold their house and moved away. I found myself hoping that they moved to a world where joblessness does not cost one his or her friends.

PROVERBS **19:4**

Wealth brings many friends,
  but the poor are left friendless.

THE SEARCH FOR GOD

When people tell me that they are looking for God, I often think that they are looking for the right definition or way of speaking about God.

Perhaps a better path is to discover what we know to be good and then to wonder where that goodness comes from.

LUKE **18:19**

Jesus said to him, "Why do you call me good? No one is good but God alone."

GIFTS FREELY GIVEN

I sit in the woods at the monastery and listen and watch the symphony of life, the reciprocity that abounds. Something as mundane as a cat covering its droppings with pine needles is a window to an intelligence that imbues all things. Someone made it all; someone is guiding it all; and all of it is a gift freely given.

I walk back to the main building, careful to avoid the little mounds of pine needles that I now observe everywhere. I go to my pew in the church and ask God that I might be grateful for those things about myself that I discreetly try to cover up. There's goodness in that stuff, too.

1 CORINTHIANS 4:7

What do you have that you did not receive? And if you received it, why do you boast as if it were not a gift?

Movement in Paradise

One thing I find heartening is the idea that there might be movement in Paradise: comings and goings, departures and arrivals, and perhaps even music—the movement of notes and the surge of the symphonic. Far from being static, perhaps God's realm moves, shifts, and changes.

Psalm **69:34-36**

Let heaven and earth praise him,
the seas and everything that moves
in them.
For God will save Zion
and rebuild the cities of Judah;
and his servants shall live there and
possess it;
the children of his servants shall
inherit it,
and those who love his name shall
live in it.

A WORRIED MAN

I was walking behind the retreat house, mulling
things over. I had a lot of worries on my mind.

Three kittens and their mother appeared right beside
the road. I was elated to make their acquaintance.
My whole outlook changed in that instant. Worries
were gone and mulling set aside for another day.

PSALM 55:22

Cast your burden on the LORD,
    and he will sustain you.

Let Nature Speak

In the mornings when I sit in the woods on the monastery grounds, I look about me and there is much to absorb. The leaves, the wind, the birds, the insects. I sense that nature has many voices that have much to teach, if I am patient enough to let them speak to me.

Job 12:7-8

"But ask the animals, and they will
teach you;
the birds of the air, and they will tell
you;
ask the plants of the earth, and they will
teach you;
and the fish of the sea will declare
to you."

THE JOY OF SIX

A friend of mine who is the mother of six said that while giving birth is painful, raising six kids is no day at the beach, either. But after she and her husband watched their children grow into decent, loving adults, she told me that the joy was well worth the various trials and tribulations they had experienced.

JOHN **16:21**

When a woman is in labor, she has pain, because her hour has come. But when her child is born, she no longer remembers the anguish because of the joy of having brought a human being into the world.

Blind Sighted

A blind man visits the monastery every year. He must be led everywhere. His need for others is so complete that he must stretch out his hand and wait for someone to help him. In his darkness, he is always provided a light by others.

How often I want to be a light unto myself and resist any kind of help. I am grateful to that blind man for what he enabled me to see.

Isaiah 42:16

I will lead the blind
   by a road they do not know,
by paths they have not known
   I will guide them.
I will turn the darkness before them
     into light,
   the rough places into level ground.
These are the things I will do,
   and I will not forsake them.

Nothing but the Truth

There have been times when I actually assumed that the whole truth existed somewhere that I could access—in a book, a program, a person.

I now accept the fact that the truth exists, but it is not at my beck and call. The truth will find me, and it will set me free.

JOHN **16:12**

"I still have many things to say to you, but you cannot hear them now."

The Finer Things

The night before Thanksgiving many years ago, I went to an Italian restaurant to order a takeout dinner. A neighborhood homeless man stood next to me. I lit up a cigarette, and he asked me for one. I gave him two. He asked me for money, and I declined, saying that I did not give money.

I left, but then I felt bad. I went back to the restaurant and asked the waitress to let the guy order whatever he wanted. I told her I would take care of it.

On the way out, I went over to him, offered him another cigarette—which he gladly took—and apologized to him for not giving him the money. I told him that he could have dinner that night and the next, free of charge. All he had to do, I said, was order what he wanted. He looked at me, thought for a second or two, and with a sniff said, "Thanks, man. But I don't like the crap they serve here. I am used to finer fare."

Then he turned and walked away.

PROVERBS 13:7

> Some pretend to be rich,
> yet have nothing;
> others pretend to be poor,
> yet have great wealth.

THANKSGIVING

At the heart of being—of existence—is sharing.
Humans are not human who do not give of themselves to others. We call the cruel, selfish person
inhuman. I am thankful this day for the human beings
in my life.

All of you share in God's grace with me.

THE GREAT AWAKENING

I gave a fellow monk a book to read that I had found insightful. When he finished it, I asked how he liked it. He said he loved the book—that it had awakened in him a deeper love and longing for God. I was happy to have played a small part in this great awakening.

JOHN 11:11

After saying this, he told them, "Our friend Lazarus has fallen asleep, but I am going there to awaken him.

THE KNITTING NEEDLES

My grandmother knit me a sweater many years ago, and I still wear it on cold winter days. I have a photo of her holding the needles as the sweater takes shape. Out of love, she created something out of nothing for me.

I picture God with those same needles, fashioning each of us in a unique design, knitting us together with tender love.

JOB **10:11**

You clothed me with skin and flesh
        and knit me together with bones and
                sinews.

FIRST FRIENDS

When I was a parish priest, I would watch the first graders on their way to the first day of school moving from the arms, tears, and kisses of their mothers or fathers to a whole new daunting world. That world soon became pleasurable in that most sacred of events: the making of friends.

JOHN 15:15

"I do not call you servants any longer, because the servant does not know what the master is doing; but I have called you friends, because I have made known to you everything that I have heard from my Father."

The Sweet and the Bitter

When I was very young and came down with a fever, Mom would crush an aspirin into a banana and mix it. It was the only way I would take medicine. I did not like pills and gave her a hard time when it came time to swallow one. So she, like many mothers, devised the banana trick and it worked. Even though I could taste the chalky residue of the aspirin, the sweetness of the banana outweighed the bitterness of the pills.

That was a long time ago. I take pills without a thought these days. No sweetening is necessary. But some things I still find hard to swallow. For example, human love does not always go down easily. There can be a bitterness and an awful aftertaste when we love with tired hearts and simply do not feel like giving.

God sometimes separates the bitter from the sweet, so that the sweetness comes later and is in ways all the richer. When it does come, I try to remember it is the genuine fruit of the ordinary salty days that life brings.

Proverbs 27:7

The sated appetite spurns honey,
but to a ravenous appetite
even the bitter is sweet.

THE BOTTLE OF VINEGAR

It was my first trip to the store by myself. I was only seven or eight, and Mom wanted a bottle of vinegar. She gave me exact change and wrote a note for the grocery man. I put the note and the money in my pocket and was off. It was a hot summer day, and the store was not far from our house.

The grocer smiled and wrapped the bottle in paper and put it in a bag. I left the store feeling very proud of myself and started for home. Not far along the way, however, I dropped the bag. With a bursting pop it hit the sidewalk. The light brown paper turned dark as the vinegar leaked and formed a puddle at my feet. I started to cry with the realization that I had messed up my first trip helping Mom.

I ran back to the store. Before I could explain what had happened, the man had already wrapped another bottle and gave it to me. "Walk slowly this time," he said. I thanked him, grabbed the bag, and with careful steps made my way to the top of my street. I was so happy that I ran the rest of the way home. I did not drop the new bottle.

The grocery man had turned that second bottle of vinegar into gold.

JOB 10:12

You have granted me life and steadfast love
and your care has preserved my spirit.

STREET LIFE

I grew up on a dead-end street with a lot of kids.

Tommy had a limp. Jimmy had a club foot. Sharon had a scar on her leg from a burn. Gary had a cleft lip. Tom never grew. Bobby had asthma. Mark was fat. Maureen was spoiled. Arthur was strange. Steve was a bully. Johnny was Jewish. Kerry never went to church. Michael was clumsy. Lynn was boy-crazy. Helen hated boys. Harold was rich. Terry was poor. Nancy liked horses. Billy liked fights. Penelope liked poodles. Regina liked sitting on the washing machine.

We kids all got along. Summer nights seemed to go on forever. It was an in-your-face existence. We sat beneath trees and played in the street. We sold lemonade to passersby and rode bikes and homemade go-carts. We played hopscotch and all sorts of street games.

We were used to being different, each in his or her own way. It did not seem to matter back then.

In some ways, I wish it stayed that way as we grew older.

MATTHEW 19:14

"Let the little children come to me, and do not stop them; for it is to such as these that the kingdom of heaven belongs."

STOCKING STUFFERS

My mother treasured the ten stockings that we strung over the fireplace each Christmas. They were among the few things that she wanted to keep for life. They held as many memories as they did candies and small toys over the years.

When we moved, she placed them in a large box in the garage for storage. The garbage collectors took the box by mistake and drove off. When Mom discovered the loss, she was near tears.

But the love and memories that filled those stockings could never be lost. It is because of that love that I now have a full heart.

LUKE 12:34

"For where your treasure is, there your heart will be also."

ALL EARS

The first word in the Rule of Saint Benedict is *Listen*.
It is an invitation to which we monks respond.

PROVERBS **4:20-22**

My child, be attentive to my words;
    incline your ear to my sayings.
Do not let them escape from your sight;
    keep them within your heart.
For they are life to those who find them,
    and healing to all their flesh.

BROTHER DWYER

I received a letter from Brother Dwyer, my high school English teacher. He liked an essay I had written and was kind enough to let me know. I wrote him back and told him how well I remembered his love for literature, especially the works of Graham Greene.

I wonder what Brother Dwyer reads these days. I should ask him.

---

2 CORINTHIANS 3:2

You yourselves are our letter, written on our hearts, to be known and read by all.

Night Sky

On a clear night in Conyers, Georgia, I can gaze into eternity.

The silent heavens are no less communicative than words. Their grandeur commands me to be still and watch. Slowly the night sky comforts me and helps me to trust in a God who cares for mere mortals.

PSALM 8:3-4

When I look at your heavens,
    the work of your fingers,
  the moon and the stars
    that you have established;
what are human beings that you
  are mindful of them,
mortals that you care for them?

SEEING GOD

As day unfolds, God will reveal something of the nature of the divine through the people around you. You will witness anger, forgetfulness, love, hope, forbearance, competence, confidence, and vulnerability in the many lives that cross your path today. Take a good look at these people and know that you have seen the face of God.

REVELATION 22:4

They will see his face, and his name will be on their foreheads.

SAYING OUR GOOD-BYES

When we were kids, Mom and Dad made sure we always introduced ourselves to guests at our house. Over the years, many related social graces sunk in: introducing others, phone manners, thank you notes, and so on.

I have never been good at saying my good-byes, however. I didn't have much need to when I was younger, and now—as I my attachment to people, places, and things has grown—the pain of saying good-bye is great.

It is sheer grace that allows me to say good-bye to the old and embrace the new with gratitude.

1 THESSALONIANS 5:16-18

Rejoice always, pray without ceasing, give thanks in all circumstances; for this is the will of God in Christ Jesus for you.

Open Season

Trees must be open to the wind, rain, sun, soil—
every season and all of time. They have no
choice.

Humans can decide whether or not to be open to
the elements. Pray each day for the wisdom to
know when to stand in the rain or snow and when
to seek shelter.

Psalm 91:1-2

> You who live in the shelter of the Most
>   High,
>   who abide in the shadow of the
>   Almighty,
> Will say to the Lord, "My refuge and
>   my fortress;
>   my God, in whom I trust."

LIFE IN THE FAST LANE

Try as we might to keep to the safe and sure lane of life, God has a way of forcing us at times into the fast lane. Best then to just step on the gas and let the world fly by, with one eye on the road and the other searching for the next exit.

1 THESSALONIANS 3:11

May our God and Father himself and our Lord Jesus direct our way.

THE GIFT SHOP

I would love to work in a gift shop during Advent. I picture strangers coming in looking for a special Christmas gift for a loved one. I would help them find it and wrap it in beautiful paper—the finest paper I could find—with colors of green and blue, red and gold. I would use fancy ribbons and nestle within each bow a surprise treasure such as candy or a tiny Christmas ornament. I would offer warm words and hot coffee to these strangers on a cold wintry day in the hope of making new friends.

EPHESIANS 4:8

"When he ascended on high he made captivity itself a captive;
he gave gifts to his people."

MAKES SENSE

Most, if not all, of my schooling was based on the rarely questioned assumption that things make sense. Studies of history, science, math, languages—even theology—carried with them the implicit expectation that an order exists to everything.

But I have learned that's not how things operate. Life is a mystery that can be lived only in faith, endured only with hope, and truly redeemed only through love.

That may be "nonsense" to some, but life demands nothing less than total trust in God, even when things don't appear to make sense.

ISAIAH **55:8**

For my thoughts are not your thoughts,
    nor are your ways my ways, says the
        LORD.

The Right Word

The late novelist J.F. Powers used to sit and stare out his office window for hours at a time looking for just the right word for a novel or an essay he was writing. The word might take a long time to come, but eventually it would arrive and he would immediately know it.

Many of us cannot understand waiting for hours for one word. But that one word might make the difference in a sentence, and the sentence in the paragraph, and the paragraph in the narrative.

God waited, and spoke the Word. God waited again, and you were born.

Job 32:11

> "See, I waited for your words,
>   I listened for your wise sayings,
>   while you searched out what to say."

Wishes

I have wished for many things in my life. I have often wondered whether what I wish for is good. The times when I have truly been called to be a better person have been painful and, at least initially, rarely something I wished for. Perhaps those are the times that God's wishes for me—instead of my own—have come true.

John 15:7

"If you abide in me, and my words abide in you, ask for whatever you wish, and it will be done for you."

What Is God (Really) Like?

We humans like to think about what God is like. Over the centuries, we have had some very lofty thoughts on this topic. They fill millions of volumes.

As far as we know, Jesus never tackled the "what-is-God-like" issue directly. When pressed about his Father in heaven, he told parables that gave some inklings but were not very specific.

So, what is God really like? I don't know, either, but if you love what you do, whomever you are with, and wherever you go today, I'll bet the question will be there—as will the answer.

Matthew 28:20

"And remember, I am with you always, to the end of the age."

Possessions

Ours is a culture that for many provides much. From the time we are very young, it is easy to appropriate the unquestioned assumptions that we deserve the best things that life has to offer and that once we get them we have the right to hold on to them.

Yet those things that make us human—that both form and inform a human heart—are not ever to be kept. Nor are they deserved. Hope, goodness, trust, love, honesty, care, simplicity, single-heartedness: these are gifts we will never own. When received, they flourish to the extent that they are shared. They multiply to the extent that we offer them to others.

LUKE **6:45**

"The good person out of the good treasure of the heart produces good, and the evil person out of evil treasure produces evil; for it is out of the abundance of the heart that the mouth speaks."

STRANGER'S WELCOME

New place, new people, nothing familiar—such an experience happens to us all at one time or another. It takes a while to get our footing. I thank God for the people who reach out to strangers and soften the edge of the new with their kindness, especially around the holiday season.

DEUTERONOMY **10:19**

You shall also love the stranger, for you were strangers in the land of Egypt.

THE HANDKERCHIEF

More than forty years ago, I was sitting in church and had a runny nose and no handkerchief. I kept sniffling and sniffling. I felt a tap on my shoulder and turned around. The woman sitting behind me smiled and gave me a handkerchief. "Keep it," she whispered. Her pretty face framed by bright red hair and her simple act of kindness is a memory that stands out from my youthful church-going years.

I am thankful that God has a way of programming my heart so that I remember such sweet gestures that knit us human beings together.

1 CHRONICLES 12:17

David went out to meet them and said to them, "If you have come to me in friendship, to help me, then my heart will be knit to you."

ALLURING DETAILS

Everyone loves a good love story—the allure, the flutter of heart, the sweet nothings whispered.

Our God is love. Thus, in every moment we are being drawn into God's embrace. History is one long swoon. Go ahead and let God sweep you off your feet.

HOSEA 2:14

Therefore, I will now allure her,
    and bring her into the wilderness,
    and speak tenderly to her.

On the Look Out

We go about our lives searching and straining to find significance, to be somebody, to secure lasting meaning. But maybe what most signifies is the search itself.

MATTHEW **6:33**

"Strive first for the kingdom of God and his righteousness, and all these things will be given to you as well."

WHAT MANNER OF GOD IS THIS?

Jesus was raised in a home with a mother and father in an ordinary town. To think that God was once a kid, playing in a street, astounds me.

MATTHEW 1:24-25

When Joseph awoke from sleep, he did as the angel of the Lord commanded him; he took her as his wife but had no marital relations with her until she had borne a son; and he named him Jesus.

Rapt in Gifts

While walking though the large basement of the
monastery church, I spotted movement out of the
corner of my eye. Turning to look, I saw Michael,
our cook, wrapping his Christmas presents as he
hid away from the rest of the community. He was
taking such care as he wrapped that he did not
notice me. He wanted the gifts to be a surprise.

This encounter gave me an image of God hiding
deep within the earth, wrapping gift after gift—gifts
without number—and sending them up throughout
the earth: beauty and goodness, trees and babies,
cities and centuries, saints and sinners.

Sirach **43:31-32**

Who has seen him and can describe
    him?
    Or who can extol him as he is?
Many things greater than these lie
    hidden,
      for I have seen but few of his
    works.

CHRISTMAS EXPECTATIONS

Christmas Eve brims with expectation. As a child, I lay awake in bed with so much swimming in my head—images of the toys that would be under the tree for my brothers and sisters and me, love for my parents, and great happiness for the times our family would spend together.

As an adult my horizons have expanded, and now my head swirls with hopes for peace and joy for all. I pray that I do what I can to hasten the coming of these things. I wait in hope for the coming of love.

HOSEA **12:6**

> But as for you, return to your God,
>   hold fast to love and justice,
>   and wait continually for your God.

THE CRY OF HOPE

Here in this monastery in Conyers, Georgia, I draw as close as I have ever known to the warm mystery that is the birth of Jesus. The singular cry of a baby gave hope a language.

LUKE 2:10

The angel said to them, "Do not be afraid; for see—I am bringing you good news of great joy for all the people."

Silent Nights

We put a great deal of work into Christmas celebrations at the monastery. By the time the big day arrives, we are all tired and looking forward to some rest. There are many things to do: songs to learn, decorations to put up, schedules to keep, meetings to attend, cards to answer, meals to cook.

In the midst of the chaos this year, I went behind the barn to sit and relax. Two cats were chasing each other back and forth. It was a mild day, and the breezes were gently nudging the limbs of the trees. Taking a deep breath of cool winter air, I realized why that first Christmas was such a humble one.

Each of us longs for peaceful, silent nights—even God.

Luke 2:15

When the angels had left them and gone into heaven, the shepherds said to one another, "Let us go now to Bethlehem and see this thing that has taken place, which the Lord has made known to us."

Snow Flakes

No two flakes of snow are alike, scientists tell us. Magnified many times, each flake is a unique pattern of dazzling beauty. I used to think about that when I would scoop a handful of snow and hold it in my palm. Of course, now that I live in Georgia, that doesn't happen very often, so I look for uniqueness in each person I meet.

Wonderful is the faith that tells us that each of us is held in the palm of God's hand and that every hair on our heads has been counted.

Wisdom 7:22

There is in her a spirit that is intelligent, holy, unique, manifold, subtle, mobile, clear, unpolluted, distinct, invulnerable, loving the good, keen, irresistible, beneficent, humane, steadfast, sure, free from anxiety, all-powerful, overseeing all, and penetrating through all spirits that are intelligent, pure, and altogether subtle.

DRINK DEEPLY

In the spring of our lives, we make our commitments with a full heart and willingness to drink of the cup of fidelity. But each year carries with it bitter disappointments, and our expectations are choked by things that happen beyond our control. As the autumn and winter bear heavy upon us, it is understandable that we may begin to look for a cup that offers a more pleasurable drink.

To live true to our commitments and say "yes" to all that happens is to welcome the God who comes in unlikely places and unexpected times. Over time through God's grace, we learn to sense the divine presence in our winters as well as our springs, and we drink willingly from the cup that has been given us.

MATTHEW 20:22

Jesus answered, "You do not know what you are asking. Are you able to drink the cup that I am about to drink?" They said to him, "We are able."

God's Work

We plan our days, our years, our lives. We expect a plentiful return on our labor: comfort, happiness, meaning, success.

In our life's work, however, what is the labor of God? Would we be pleased if we knew the answer?

1 Corinthians 3:7

So neither the one who plants nor the one who waters is anything, but only God who gives the growth.